COVER STORY
Album Cover Art

ISBN 978-1-57687-509-4

Wax Poetics Books
45 Main Street, Suite 224
Brooklyn, NY 11201

waxpoeticsbooks.com

Distributed by powerHouse Books
37 Main Street
Brooklyn NY, 11201

powerHouseBooks.com

To order please contact Wes Del Val:
T 212 604 9074 x 103
F 212 366 5247
E wes@powerHouseBooks.com

Printed in China

PUMA®
puma.com

waxpoetics

PREFACE

by Brian DiGenti

Through manifest destiny, records have a way of finding new, true owners. We create unique relationships with used records, depending on their covers, their sounds, and—sometimes more importantly—where they came from or how we found them. Usually, simply being in the right place at the right time creates a profound sense of analogy that can outweigh any prior ownership. This brought me to a vision of a different type of album cover book—personal, yet mysterious. **Wax Poetics** contributors were given the assignment to choose twenty albums and pair them up. The only guidelines were that the albums should speak (not necessarily sing) to them—via the cover, the music, or the alchemical symbiosis created through vinyl thaumaturgy that every good collector practices. Easy like Sunday morn.

One summer, many years ago, I was practicing the black-platter arts myself, visiting estate sales in the country(club)side of San Diego's North County. In a near-empty garage, a box of typical record-club classical albums obscured a group of roughly twenty sealed copies of Kit Ream's *All That I Am*. In a moment of hurried decision-making, I bought two copies and swore I'd return the following day if I liked what I heard. Being pre-blog days, there was no info to be found on the Internet, and a quick needle-drop did not illuminate its hidden messages. The two copies were quickly forgotten about. Several years later, I came across the albums in my collection. This time, I paid close attention as its magick was imparted; revelation followed. The Internet soon confirmed that I was not alone with my anagogical obsession with this analog. But my relationship with the record deepened when I soon learned that those twenty sealed copies had been sitting in the garage of Mr. Ream's deceased blood relative—and now they were likely in a landfill, awaiting future archaeology.

Sometimes, the relationship we have with a record is due to a prior contact someone else had with the same record. Take, for example, the handwritten inscription "May you never lose" on

James Mason's *Rhythm of Life*. The record would end up in the garbage on Broadway and 12th in Manhattan before finding its final home with **Jeff "Chairman" Mao**, who says, "Given the dedication written on that album cover, there was always something very melancholy to me about the fact that it wound up there." Another interesting find came when Mao was working on *ego trip's Book of Rap Lists* and made a run to Boston for secondhand CDs. The L.A. Team 12-inch he found there had the familiar scrawl of *Source* magazine cofounder Jon Shecter, stating a disdain for West Coast rap and citing proof of East Coast dominance by the record's use of "too much emulator."

An album can be a sign of the times without the help of its owner's graffiti. The artwork itself can be social barometer. Editor-in-chief **Andre Torres** focuses a critical eye on Bwana's eponymous release. "It represents everything right and wrong about a good record cover," he explains. What's right about it, he says, is the artwork and design. "It's simple and very effective as an image sitting in that twelve-inch square space." Then there's the image itself. "An undoubtedly racist portrayal of someone of African descent. It's both fun and naïve and horribly wrong and racist all at once. It seems to hang in a netherworld of racial indifference where the image simply exists, and only in the viewer's heart and mind does this image actually 'mean' anything."

Contributing editor **Andrew "Monk One" Mason** knows how whimsical records can be. As a club DJ, he's seen plenty of covers. *Salsaaa!!* features a photo of a young lady pouring—of all things—ketchup onto a pile of records. While it may not look as appetizing as Mongo's *Sofrito*, it's actually a compilation of classic Fania salsa—with a "crazy hyped-up disc jockey introducing each song," says Mason. "Really funny. But the music is great."

Contributing editor **Dante Carfagna** has helped shed light on American (especially Midwest) private press records. John Bayley's *Minstrel of the Morning* (look for the kid in lotus position)

offers a glimpse into this endlessly mysterious world. First encountered in a thrift store in Kansas City, "the cover was so unique and mystifying that me and some friends had developed an entire mythology as to the why and where." That imagined mythology was soon shattered when his girlfriend's musician father saw the LP at his house and said matter-of-factly, "Oh, the John Bayley LP. I played this kid's sixteenth birthday party," bringing the photo's subjects back to a more banal plane of existence. Still, Carfagna points to this record as an example of when a great cover can elevate otherwise shoulder-shrugging music—Christian reggae rock.

Some people have the good fortune of having great records handed down to them from their parents or a grandfather. Others aren't so lucky. **Amir Abdullah**, with his partner Kon, DJs around the world, all the while looking for new sounds to add to the deep-crate repertoire. But the intimate records are always closest to home. Amir was introduced to his favorite jazz artist, pianist Horace Silver, by his pops. But it took him over twelve years to locate an original copy of *The Stylings of Silver* for himself. "My father has the record, but he wouldn't let me have it, so I had to find my own copy," Amir says. "You just hear his pure genius."

Contributing editor **Matt Rogers** spends most of his time on the chitlin circuit, filming and interviewing B-3 organ players for his documentary. The cover of Jimmy McGriff and Groove Holmes's *Giants of the Organ in Concert* has the small-stage intimacy of Rogers's local Harlem haunts like the American Legion. McGriff—who Rogers spent weeks interviewing for Issue 11 and 12—was once a student of Holmes. Here, they share the stage as equals—and share their experience directly with the audience.

Contributing writer **Oliver Wang**, our resident PhD, has typed millions of words while reporting on music over the past decade, whether for magazines, books, or his blog. Being a man of letters that he is, it's no wonder he chose the hand-lettered cover of Larry T. and the Family's *I'm Moving On*. "There is something about the sheer simplicity of this cover—the use of fonts to define its character, the lack of visual clutter—that says to me, 'I'm either a wack children's record or something special that you need to pay attention to,'" Wang says. "Luckily, it's the latter."

Writer **Robbie Busch** is also a painter. His eye was immediately drawn to Sparrow's Troubadours' *Hot & Sweet*. This calypso-with-heat record sports a "clean, simple late-'60s design. I love the simplified, cartoony sparrows and the primary colors," he says. It's always great when you can judge a record by its cover. "The real treat is their take on the Young Holt Unlimited classic 'Soulful Strut.' After about three minutes, they give the drummer some, and he takes it to a whole other level, turning a workout on a standard into a masterful breaks classic."

Photographer **Brian Cross aka B+** has traveled the world to shoot his subjects—from Jamaica and Haiti for Damian Marley to Ethiopia for Mulatu—and has collected records along the way. He has also shot a few album covers over the years; his first, in 1993, was Eazy-E's notorious *It's On (Dr. Dre) 187um Killa*. Cross had first met Eazy when working on the book *It's Not About a Salary*, which helped get him this cover shoot. Cross shot sixty rolls at Eazy's mom's old house, then serving as a playhouse for Eazy. "I remember there were a lot of real guns! And that he was really cool," Cross says. "Eazy was pissed off when I showed up with the processed film. He was like, 'What do want me to do with all these?'" But Eazy was quick to find the cover. "Yeah, this says it all," Eazy said at the time, referring to his Dr. Dre dis concept. Later on, before Eazy's untimely passing, he paid B+ to teach him how to take flicks, and even participated in a Bone Thugs shoot.

Contributing editor **J. P. Jones** has gone through more records than most people ever see in their life. And he has probably already sold back the records shown here. But one record he'll always hold on to is the Lynnfield Pioneers' *Free Popcorn* (that's him behind the kit in the moon-base tower). Looking less to rock a crowd than to make them dance, the Pioneers paid homage to James Brown, KMD, Les Mogol's *Dances and Rhythms of Turkey*, and, Jones says, "the Actuel albums we hoarded." Naturally, Jones laced the album with multiple drum breaks, hoping to have young secret squirrels get their sample on.

Contributing writer **Dave Tompkins** has a serious jones for bass and electro, not to mention a historical bias towards the vocoder, which he has written extensively about in a seriously deep book, soon to be published. Explore with him Miami, America's new musical Manifest Destiny.

INTRODUCTION
PRETTY MUCH PRETTY WEIRD

by Dave Tompkins

"Any single Miami story, moreover, was hard to follow, and typically required a more extensive recall of other Miami stories." –Joan Didion, *Miami*

"That's illegal use of the illegal use" –Coach Bob Wheeler

In December of 1979, a Black insurance agent rolled through a stoplight in North Miami and popped a wheelie on his orange Kawasaki 900. He flipped off a squad car, got chased, and was fatally beaten by five members of the Dade County Public Safety Department. The officers were White and acquitted. The following May, bottles went aerial and Miami was nearly burned down to the limestone.

Fourteen-year-old Byron Smith did not participate in the ensuing eighty million dollars in damages, though he did loot a gas station for beer and cigarettes. His friend Garfield Baker stayed in and watched the riots on TV and then flipped to *Monty Python's Flying Circus*. There he saw a couch, an easy chair, a dining table, a lamp, and maybe a hat rack running a fifty-yard dash. There was no clear winner though many believed the couch was robbed.

Four years and another riot later, Smith and Baker stood behind a Haitian tailoring shop, watching a man thoughtfully break bottles. The man wore a leather Rocky the Squirrel hat and a necklace of audio patch cords with brass tips. Standing on miked concrete, he'd spent hours refining the sound of obliterated glass. It was all about tinkle separation.

Trust me, people are going to dance to this shit.

This was to be believed, because the man in the funny hat was Pretty Tony Butler, the producer/engineer behind the early Miami electro sound. The patch cords on his neck were a matter of pride not practicality, the jewelry of one who assembled this recording studio himself; it was electronically secured by the two best second-story men in Miami. The studio/label was called Music Specialists, and the patch cords were borrowed from its mixing console, which had been paid for in cash and christened with cocaine. In this sense (that being of smell), Music Specialists saw more action in Miami in 1984 than the squirrel pilot hat did in World War I.

Byron Smith and Garfield Baker had already heard about Pretty Tony, the first guy in Miami to have Space Invaders hooked up to the TV in his Oldsmobile. They knew he was captain of the Partydown DJs and that he and a spotlight expert named Everlovin' Evans were nearly sainted for bringing Planet Patrol down to Miami. (Planet Patrol was big as Bee Gees down there.) So when these two eighteen-year-olds were asked to make records with Music Specialists, they were there with florescent goggles on. No longer were they two failed high school pimps, trying to win drum-machine money at the dog track. No more making crap clock-radio demos in their bathroom. No more yelling like Run-DMC about Coast Guard coke busts. No more having to drive a rust-colored '74 Chevy Nova (called "The Tragic," because they "always ran into a motorcycle or something").

In the early '80s, Music Specialists was the only successful, independent Black-owned label making electro funk. This was at a time when doing hip-hop in Miami was, per Smith, "like UFOs." Pretty Tony had clout by proxy—he was friends with Nat Moore, All-Pro helicopter for the Miami Dolphins and owner of Superstar Rollerteque, a North Miami rink where Butler had been a resident DJ, playing "Turning Japanese" while kids skated backwards. Even more alluring, Butler was partners with Sherman Nealy, one of the biggest coke dealers out of Opa-Locka, Florida. (Opa-Locka's cinder-block projects had once stashed the Cuban Revolutionary Council—ideal for plotting a flubbed overthrow of a communist regime.) Nealy worked under Rick Brownlee, the proprietor of a twenty-one-million-dollar-a-year business that would later star in its own episode of *FBI Files*, appearing on the Discovery Channel long after both Nealy and Brownlee had been incarcerated.

For Garfield Baker and Byron Smith, teenagers who sold dollar joints in high school, this was some big-time shit.

Having records played all over the rinks, radio, parking lots, and in the JC Penny dressing room was kind of cool too. Pretty Tony was the production genius behind strip-mall electro hits like Debbie Deb's "When I Hear Music" and "Look Out Weekend." (With Debbie Deb, "Chance" always went with "dance" and she never saw so many guys despite the fog machines, lasers, Binaca mist, and shark-attack neon.) Pretty Tony had his own releases, most notably a 12-inch called "Fix It in the Mix," which featured his signature glass atomization. Butler would recycle this effect on later classics like "Party Has Just Begun" and "Jam the Box"—the latter being an unintended nod to speech scramblers and pirate radio, ever popular since the CIA moved down to Miami in the late 1950s. On "Fix It in the Mix," the damage sounded more extensive on record than it did in that back alley in Little Haiti. As if someone had tossed a coconut through your grandma's living room window and invited in all the mosquitoes and whatever rare collectible bug tarnation the hurricanes had blown in that season.

There are unseen nerdy forces at work here, especially for a guy who once used Partydown as a name brand. True to all 8,016 knobs in his studio, Tony Butler was an electronic introvert. Before Music Specialists took off, Sherman Nealy had paid for him to study engineering at the renowned Boutwell Studios in Birmingham, Alabama—under the eggheads who did sound design for the Hubble Telescope. A sonic neat freak, Butler went by his tech manuals while everything else at Music Specialists seemed to be pretty much off the books.

This was fine by Garfield Baker and Byron Smith. On Christmas Eve of 1984, they were notified that they would be the new Freestyle, the second of three versions of Freestyle that would be in circulation in Miami record stores. The first was headed by Calvin Mills II, a former jingler for the Burger King "BK Express" cheeseburger delivery van. The third was Larry Princeton, a former pimp/backup singer for Harold Melvin who sported white lizard boots and held a degree in sociology from University of Miami. To make matters more contractually wonky (and more Miami), these Freestyles were often distinct from those who performed as Freestyle. And while the name was being passed around like a bogus real estate deed in the Everglades, it helped that Music Specialists had a vocoder at its disposal to mask their identity. As Pretty Tony had once said, "You don't have to leave Miami to become somebody."

The number of Freestyles was only outnumbered by the Debbie Debs, of which there were five, possibly six, and in all colors and sizes. This included "an old-White-lady-damn-near-Debbie-Deb." Estimates varied and most were pretty whatever. At one point, the *Miami Herald* even claimed Pretty Tony was Debbie Deb. Meanwhile, the original Debbie Deb, who actually could sing, didn't want to be Debbie Deb due to stage fright.

In 1985, after much Debbie debauchery, Smith, Baker, and two guys nobody seems to know anything about recorded "Don't Stop the Rock." They suddenly found themselves on the cover of their own record, floating in front of downtown Miami in road-retardant motocross suits. Somewhat glassed in, aquariumish. A man named Sweetback Clark On Tour was in charge of the art direction but the getups were Pretty Tony's idea. It's easy to take advice from a man in a flying squirrel helmet if you have a hit record, a limo full of girls, and an endless supply of a drug that makes you feel like jumping ten moons on a tricycle and doing a No-Hander Can-Can in space. Check out those masks.

Check out how the moon is bowling up behind the skyline.

Pretty next shit.

The Hubble Telescope boys might've freaked at this lunar encroachment. ("Umm…why isn't the moon 239,000 miles from Earth where it's supposed to be?") But the new Miami skyline probably welcomed the distraction—this spurt of glass and metal had appeared just as mysteriously, not so much defying the laws of gravity as the laws of real estate. Back in '85, everything in Miami was paid for through the nose in cash. This included Freestyle's Yamaha Assault Pressure Suits. This also included "Don't Stop the Rock," a song where robots gawked at girls in translucent jeans, leather miniskirts, and whatever else the "Freakathon" called for. (The Blowcoder was truly meant for words like "Freakathon"—a Cylonotone that scrunched its nose into its brain.)

For Music Specialists, the Freakathon was moving at the speed of the bazooka-powder high. "We're talking buy-your-own-island money," said one anonymous source. "And the fleet of speedboats to get out there." Bags of cash were dropped off at the studio. The Bee Gees were calling. Radio DJs left with acetates and runny noses. The distribution warehouse was visited by the local Miami SWAT chapter. Notoriety was quickly confused for fame.

In 1985, the year "Don't Stop the Rock" was released, the City of Miami awarded Tony Butler the key to Broward County. In 1987, when Freestyle went to Los Angeles and headlined over Dr. Dre's World Class Wreckin' Cru, Tony Butler was locked up in county. He'd been busted with MC Shy D's ex-girlfriend at the Omni Hotel in Atlanta after receiving a Fed Ex containing an incriminating amount of the Colombian GNP. Inconveniently, another Tony Butler had been working in the hotel mailroom. He signed for the package and realized it wasn't baking soda. So add two Tony Butlers to the five maybe six Debbie Debs and three Freestyles and keep your receipts.

When Freestyle returned from tour, Music Specialists had been replaced by the offices of Skyywalker Records, a label run by Luther Campbell. (Campbell said Pretty Tony really "busted his bubble" when he refused to sign 2 Live Crew to Music Specialists.) Roughly a year later, Butler was out on probation and sold his catalog to Bo "Knows Where All the Bodies Are" Crane at Pandisc Records, lowballing the dream. Accounts of what really happened in this morass range from conflicting to no comment.

Among the contested was "Fix It in the Mix," a song that began with a crew of squirrel tech support in a Mayday panic, reporting problems on all channels at all frequencies and in every pitch conceivable, from Minibike Mouse with his drawers on too tight to the doofus who swallowed a tree trunk. As if someone had flipped his Lindberg lid.

Then, finally, a fat squirrel with a winter of gumballs in his jowls. "I'm trying to maintain proper stabilization on this channel without creating a situation of overmodulation."

About that overmodulation. The meticulous engineer does not want overmodulation, fearing the bass, the purple cardiac arrest of Miami rap, would "ghettoize" his sound. Overmodulation can crack a snow globe.

"The 808 was going against the laws of engineering," says Byron Smith. "Mainly to White engineers, even though Tony knew that's the sound of the ghetto where he came from. But Luke didn't give a damn. That's why he called them Ghetto Style DJs. That's why 2 Live Crew didn't get on Music Specialists. Tony was so into the theory of engineering that we had to beg him to finally let the boom go."

So the boom went, propagating.

Miami always had a rich history of booms and busts, whether real estate or bass. The one boom that survived came from a low-end property value: Liberty City Projects, the first large-scale government-funded housing in the South. Once home to Pretty Tony Butler and Luther Campbell and once nearly destroyed after the legal system had failed Black Miami yet again. Overmodulation is drastic change. Broken glass everywhere, the backwash bottom of no return.

Amid the chaos of "Fix It in the Mix," Pretty Tony decides to reverse the obliteration. Probably just because he could. The noise is sucked into the subwoofer, glass backwards, taking all hell else with it. A *voop!* in a vacuum. Bottle returns to hand. For a moment, everything is clear. As if nothing happened at all.

Based on interviews with Byron Smith, Garfield Baker, Larry Princeton, Trinere, Luther Campbell, and Allen Johnston "The Music Specialist," conducted fall of 2002 and summer of 2004. Pretty Tony now runs a successful electronic security business.

BUT THE ONE WITH THE CABINETS

That's pretty much it. For one record sleeve at least. One imagines that the other 239 covers would have something to say.

Take the girl in pink, for example, walking across that mountain of speakers.

Once Missy Mist, always Michelle Broome. She once fell in love with the guy across the page who appears to be in the advanced stages of speaker mumps. That's Speakerhead, aka Eric Griffin. He was the first to use tonal bass on record (at least one that was suggestive enough to get the sub freqs out on the dance floor). This humpbacked waveform had character and personality, the kind of bass you'd treat to lunch if only it'd stop punching you in the gut.

Arguably one of the most innovative hip-hop producers out of Miami, Griffin worked for Bass Station Records, which like Mu-

sic Specialists, was backed by kilo revenue. Broome's father, a Metro Dade detective, was unenthused about her new boyfriend, especially after the Bass Station CFO, Norberto "Candyman" Morales, was found murdered in his fishtank home. Nor would he have cared that Griffin's most famous tone, "Just Give the DJ a Break," celebrated a dance called the Toilet Bowl. Or that its bass would've humbled that mountain of speakers that appeared on his daughter's record sleeve.

A beloved local Miami DJ named Uncle Al provided the sound system for the Missy Mist cover. Sadly, Uncle Al would be murdered for his pirate radio transmitter—for his frequency, to be specific. And, sadly, Eric "Speakerhead" Griffin was killed in his recording studio in St. Louis, for reasons still unclear.

Broome said that after the photo shoot, they shuttled that speaker garrison to the National Guard Armory where Big Al threw a party. There, kids peered into the bass cabinets as if they were caves, waiting for a sine wave so deep it that it seemed to originate from the unsure ground upon which they stood. It became the very air they breathed and knocked them back smiling in their shoes.

A tough little old lady once said, "So much in Miami depends on the movement of air."

LA 30004

LIVELY ARTS

Burgess Meredith
reads
Ray Bradbury

SIR MIX-A-LOT
I'M A TRIP

b/w THE SMASH HIT!
SQUARE DANCE RAP (POWER REMIX)
PLUS...
I WANT A FREAK
MY STUDIO

REAL RAW

Drop Them Drawers

Real Raw - Drop Them Drawers
Including...
Drop Them Drawers (Remix)
Get Up and Dance
Betty (Extended Version)
Studio Rhymes

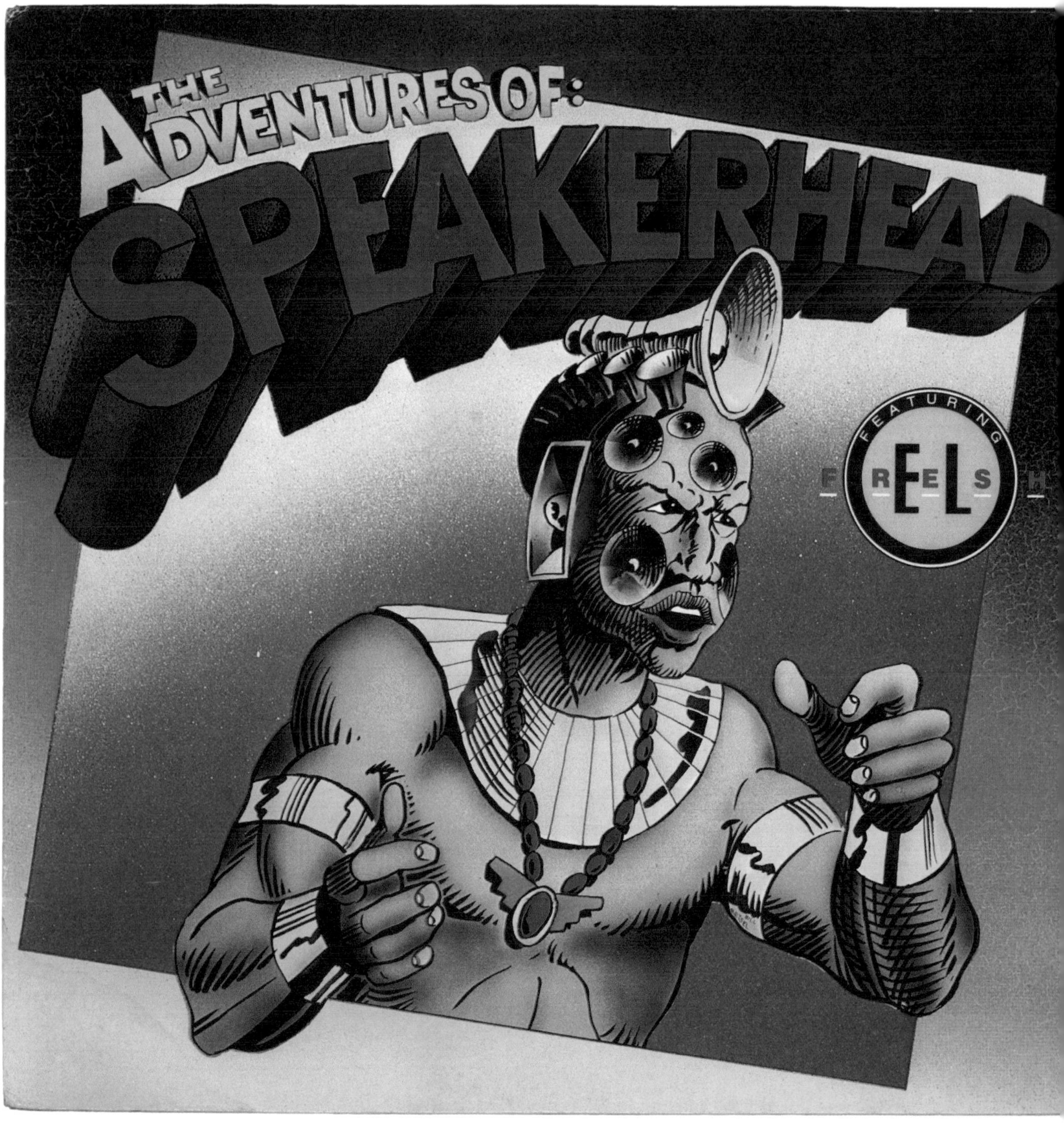

THE ADVENTURES OF:
SPEAKERHEAD
FEATURING
FRESH
E-L

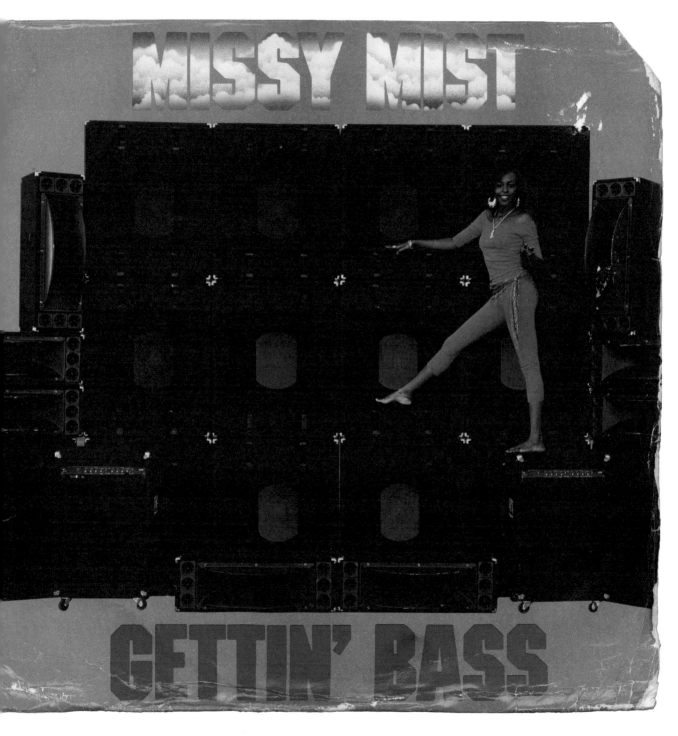

LIL' MAC

THE
LYRICAL
MIDGET

808
EIGHT—HUNDRED & EIGHT

BEATS

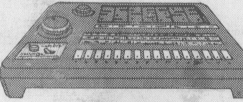

THE UnknowN DJ

Techno Hop Records
L.A. Ca.

Special Thanks to Tom Joyner and
Kyle Gibson
Tom Thompson
Pam Gibson
The Snake
Big Al
Cassandra
Kiest Park
Richard MacDonald
Ken Richardson
Daryl Geiger
Mr. K. Kold
Camp Wisdom Car Wash
MC TNT
EOAP
EZ Roc-C
Gino Dez
Def Party
Singing Hills
Bumble Bee
by Something Fresh

DOMINATING
MC's

KNOWLEDGE BOUND

THE Mix Crew
"Black Leather"

Left and Right Shoe M.C.'s
Featuring
D.J. Rated "X"

Get Funky and Get Loose
Hard Core Bass
It's Your Chance *(Capt. Hook's Bonus)*
You Turn Me On

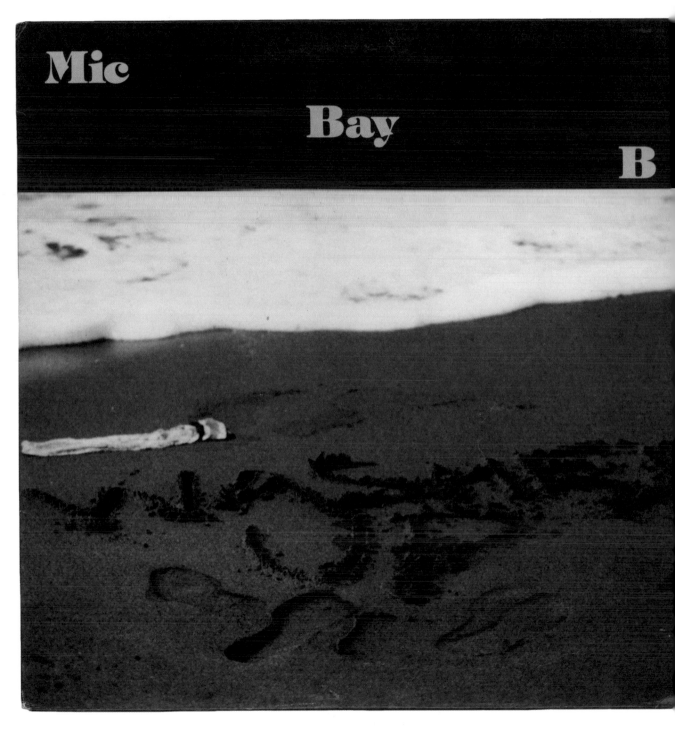

sound of joy

sun ra and the arkestra

STEREO DS-414

COMPATIBLE STEREO

GEMA

LPG-3066

EL GRAN COMBO

LOS NENES SICODÉLICOS

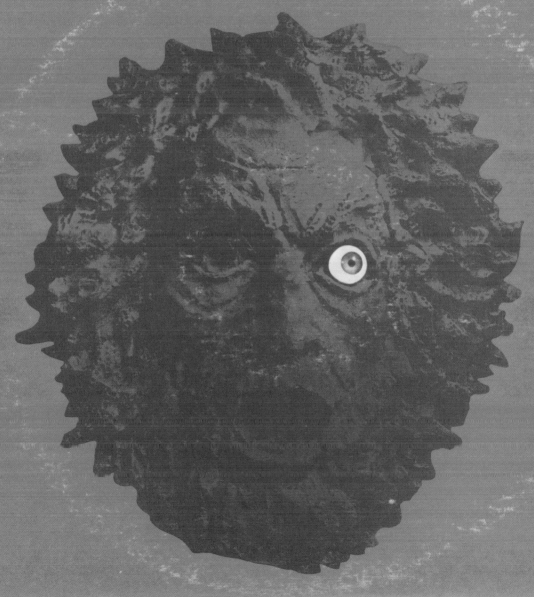

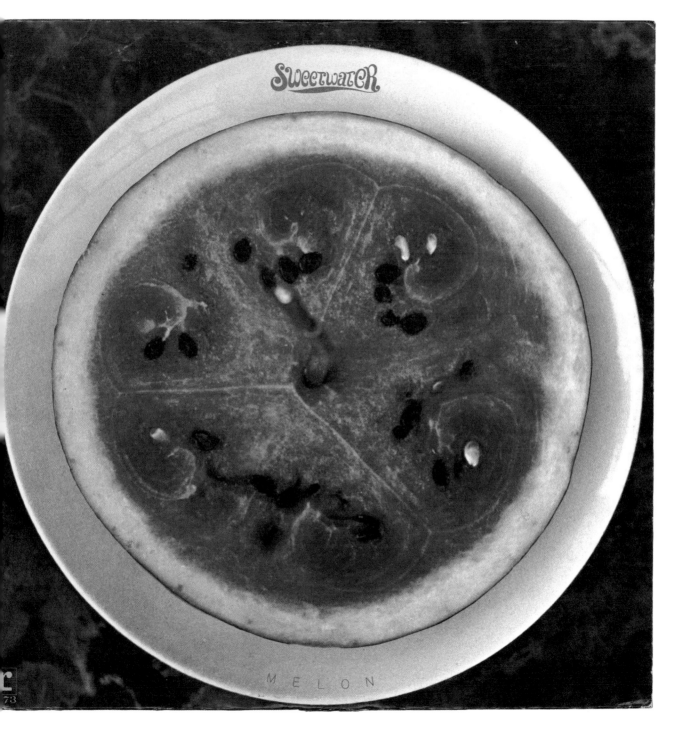

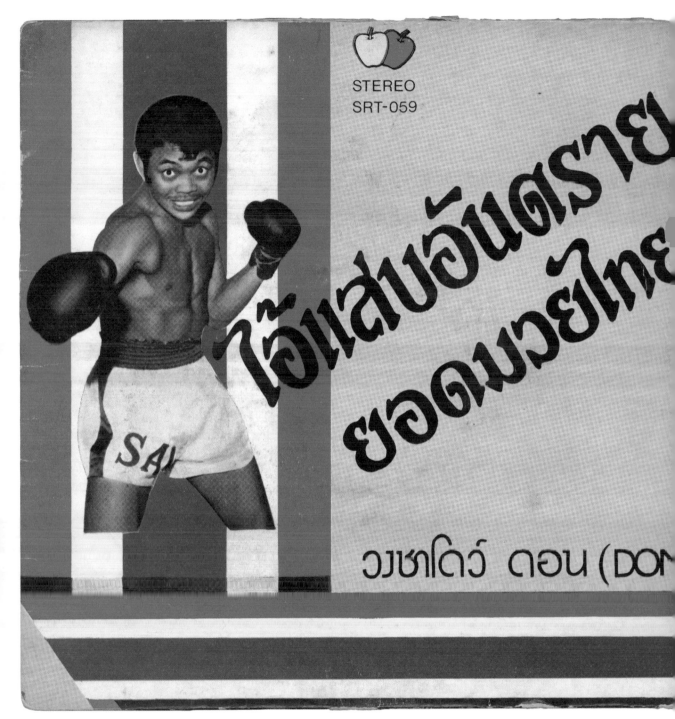

Prestige
PR 7487

FrEddiE McCOY
PEAS 'N' riCE

DESIGN/HAZ JO SCHWALBACH

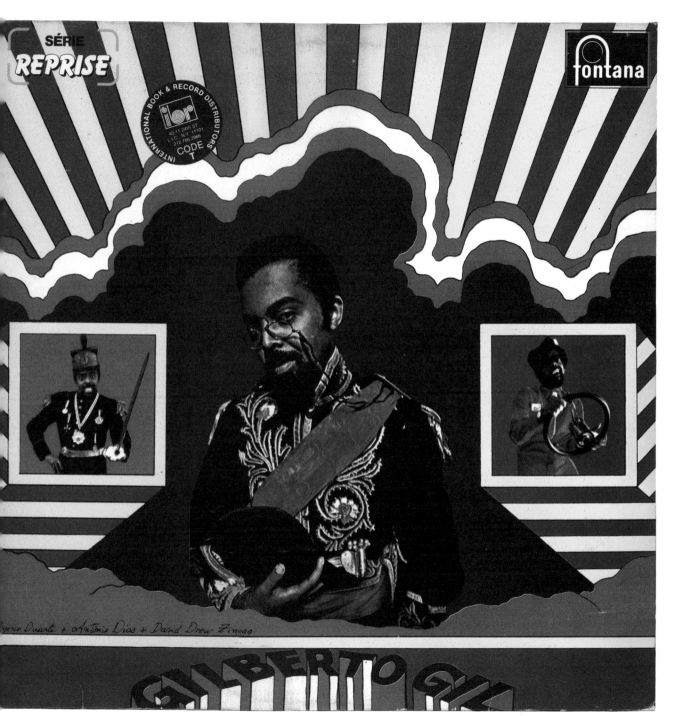

SÉRIE
REPRISE

fontana

~gerio Duarte + Antônio Dias + David Drew Zingg

GILBERTO GIL

UGLYMAN

UGLY D. J. with the rockstone voice

Ugly Lover

THIS IS OUR MUSIC

THE ORNETTE COLEMAN QUARTET

WITH DONALD CHERRY / ED BLACKWELL / CHARLIE HADEN

ATLANTIC 1353 FULL *dynamics-frequency* SPECTRUM

THE RAP PACK

HUBERT
LAWS
FAMILY

EKS-74080 STEREO

The Voices of East Harlem

RIGHT ON BE FREE

STEREO

CG 70598

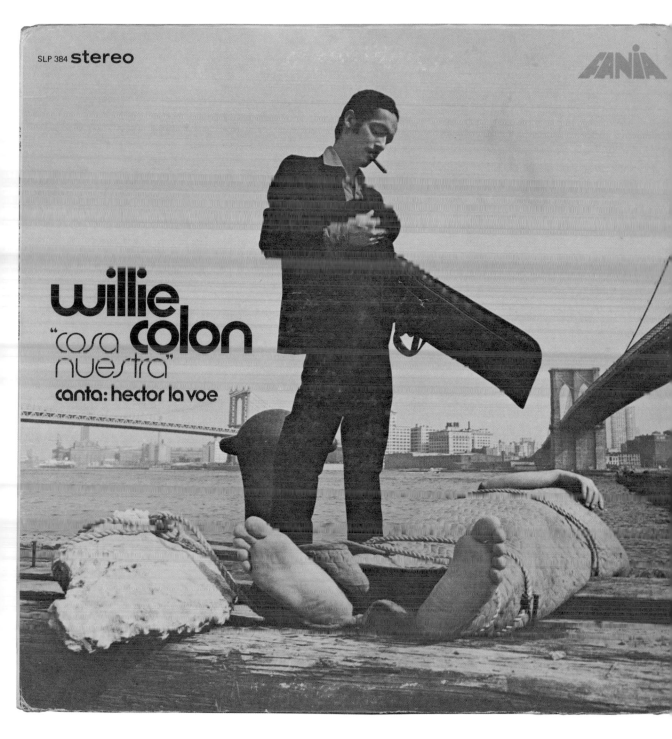

KING T

ACT A FOOL

liberated brother
weldon irvine

COMPATIBLE
stereo

ROBERTO ROENA
Y SU APOLLO SOUND 5

INTERNATIONAL

SLP 00443

lightly swiss

LATIN HUSTLE
WITH **TORO**

coco records

CLP 106
COMPATIBLE STEREO

SONO ESTEREO

DIS CON
SONO
RADIO

S.E.9412

BOMBA TROPICAL

ENRIQUE
LYNCH
Y SU
CONJUNTO

QUINN HARRIS · ALL IN THE SOUL ·

MASTERMINDS

REYNOLDS
RECORDS®

I'M MOVING ON

BY

LARRY T.

AND

THE FAMILY

FOLKWAYS RECORDS FL 9714

JUJUS
ALCHEMY OF THE BLUES
POEMS BY
SARAH WEBSTER FABIO
READ BY
SARAH WEBSTER FABIO
WITH MUSICAL BACKGROUND

MUSICOR MS 3230

SOUL

can you feel it

JA 3-26-36 **Stereo**

BAD TALK

COOKIE WONG

GOPIKRSNA GLOBAL ENTERTAINER presents

MORCHHA

CONFRONTATION OF ACTION WITH REACTION

MUSIC: BAPPI LAHIRI

Polydor

2392 202

STEREO 200870

LA
DANZA
DE LOS
MIRLOS
AFROSOUND

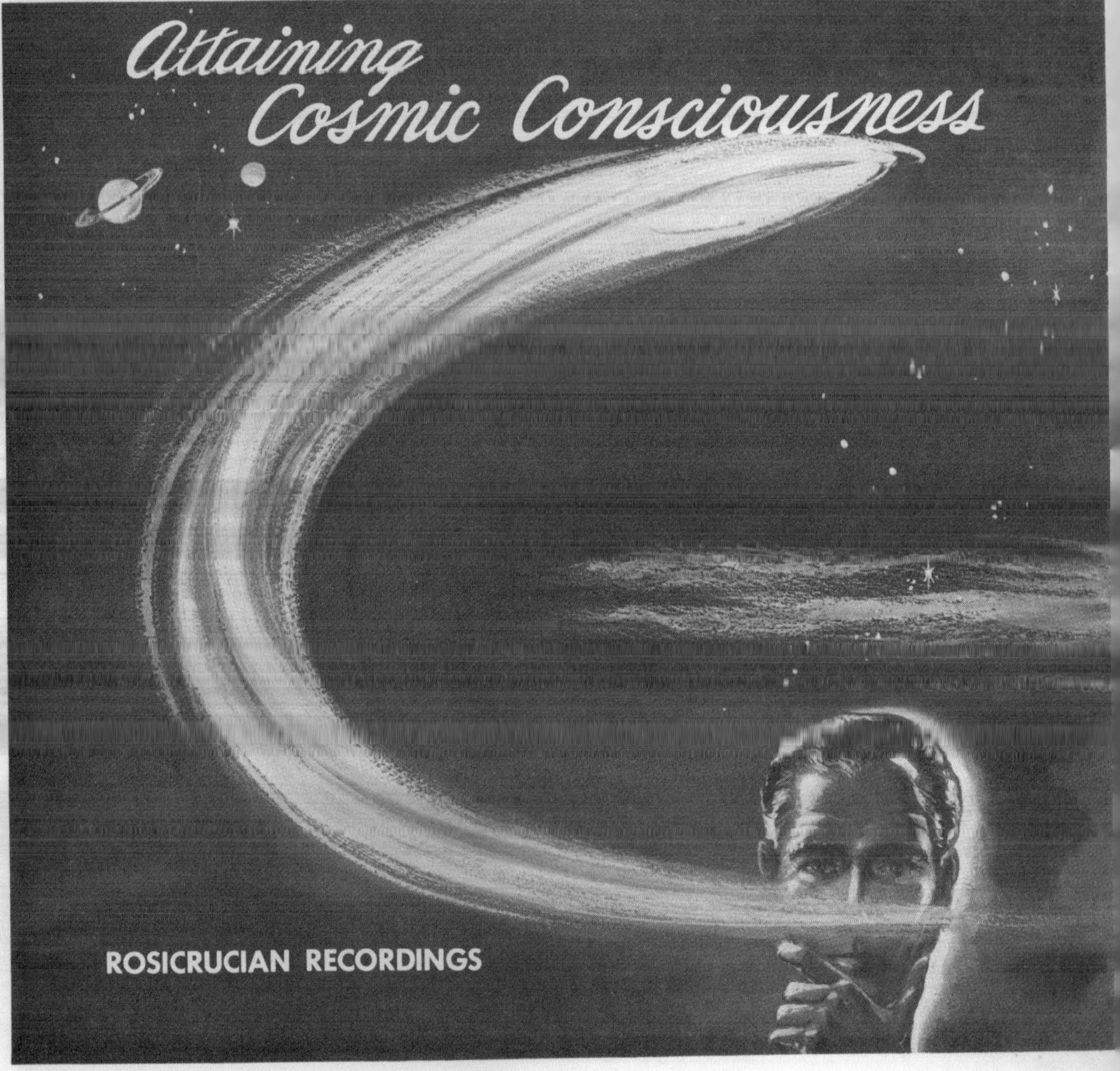
Attaining
Cosmic Consciousness
ROSICRUCIAN RECORDINGS

RECORDS
ALL MUZIC PRODUCTIONS T.M.
#1233001

MICHEL HERR

BILL FRISELL

VINTON JOHNSON

KERMIT DRISCOLL

GOOD BUDDIES

ORIGINAL MOTION PICTURE SOUNDTRACK

Music Composed and Conducted by
Les Baxter

the DUNWICH HORROR

H. P. LOVECRAFT'S
CLASSIC TALE OF
TERROR AND THE
SUPERNATURAL!

eugene mc daniels
the left rev. mc d.

headless heroes
of the apocalypse

STEREO
ATLANTIC
SD 8281

STEREO
PHIL MOORE JR.
RIGHT ON
Promotional Copy
NOT FOR SALE
SD 1530
ATLANTIC

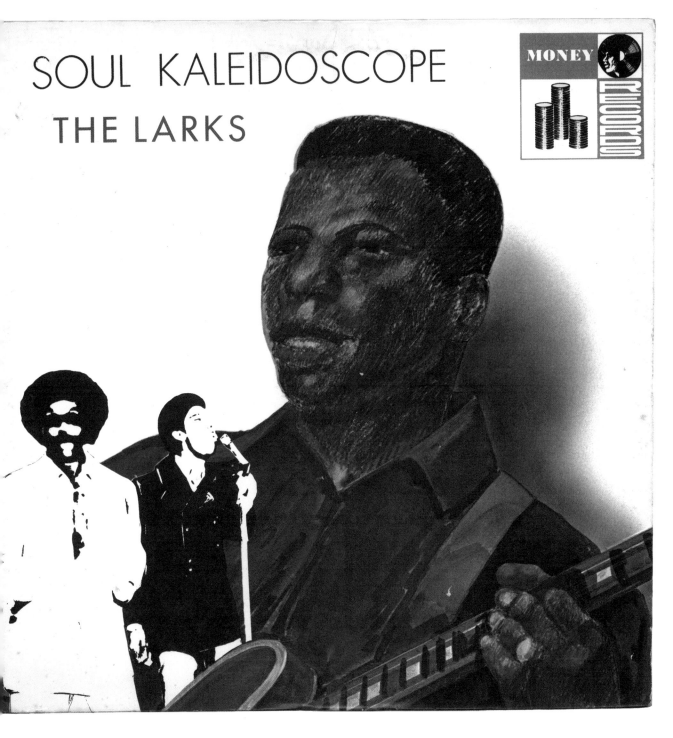

JAMES POLK & CO.

TP 100

You Know The Feeling.....!

"ALL
THAT
I
AM"

Creative Records • Kit Ream

STEREO KIL 72002

KILMARNOCK
· RECORDS

New York City

GHETTO
SUITE

Composed, conducted and produced
by the creator *of* HAIR and
TWO GENTLEMEN OF VERONA —
— GALT MACDERMOT

Vocal Interpretations: ANGELA ORTEGA

BEYOND BODY AND SOUL
SOUL GENERATION

TAPE

BDS 5079 STEREO

Stairsteps

Including:
I LOVE YOU — STOP
HUSH CHILD
EVERYBODY IS A STAR
MY SWEET LORD
SNOW

BUDDAH RECORDS
Reg. U.S. Pat. Off.

UNIVERSAL JONES

VOL.I

MV 5084

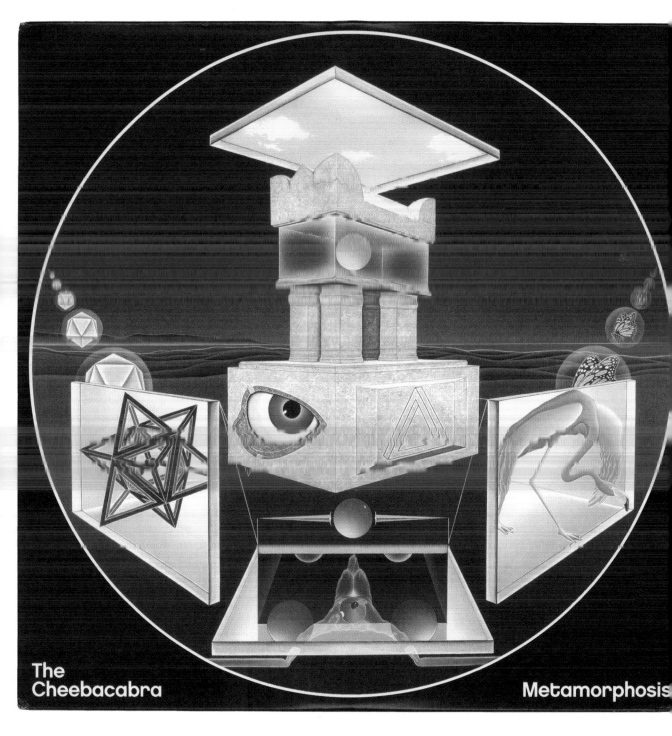

The
Cheebacabra

Metamorphosis

Cover Story **05**

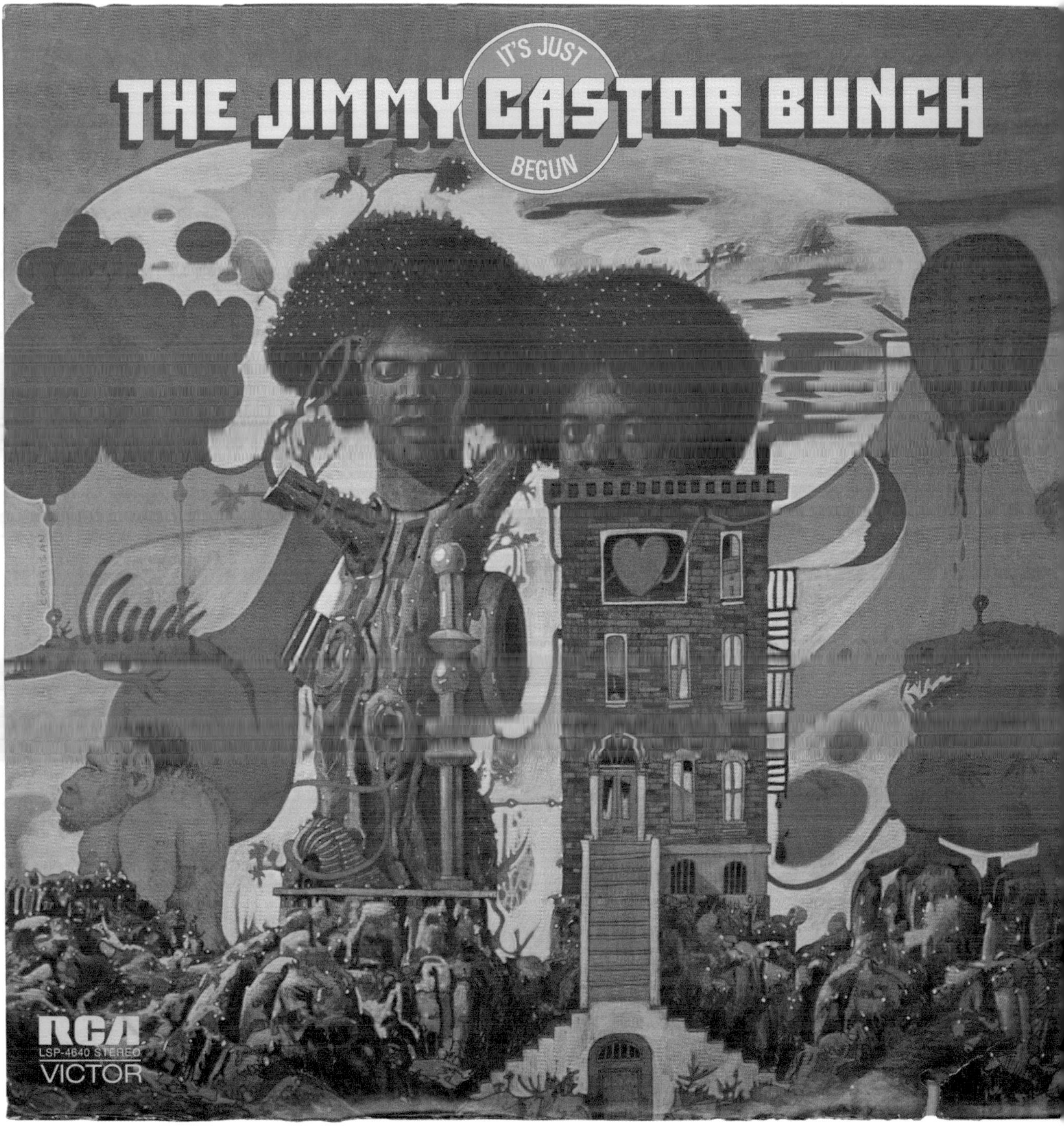
IT'S JUST
THE JIMMY CASTOR BUNCH
BEGUN
RCA
LSP-4640 STEREO
VICTOR

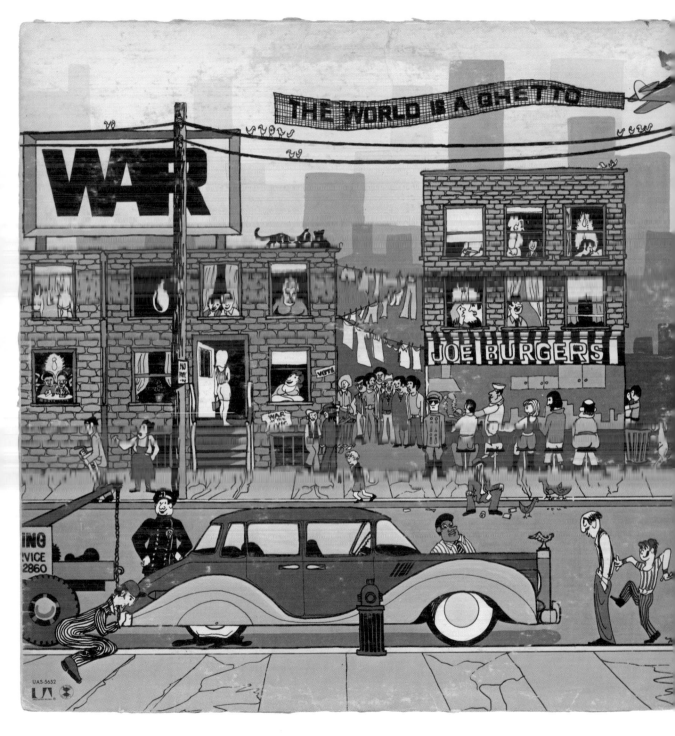

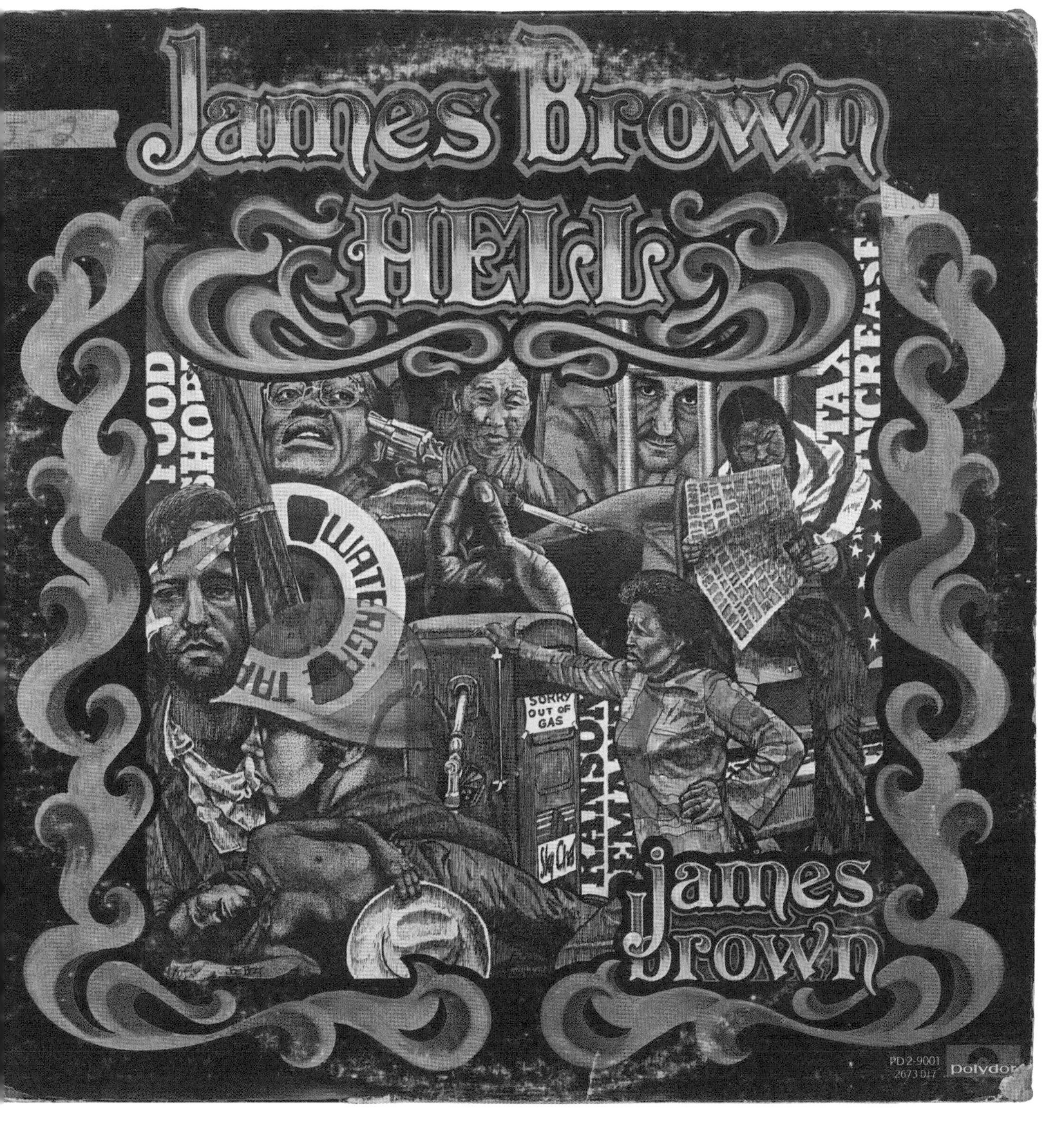

James Brown
HELL
FOOD
SHOES
TAX INCREASE
WATERGATE
SORRY OUT OF GAS
james brown
PD 2-9001
2673 017
Polydor

GM 3300

GIANTS OF THE ORGAN IN CONCERT
JIMMY McGRIFF   GROOVE HOLMES

THE COMPLETE CONCERT RECORDED LIVE AT PAUL'S MALL, BOSTON, 1973

2 RECORD SET

GROOVE MERCHANT

El Chicano Revolución

STEREO KS 3640

STEREO

ROBERTA FLACK/FIRST TAKE

SD 8230

ATLANTIC

CA-60001

CADET
STEREO

Back To The Roots / Ramsey Lewis

VOLT RECORDS
VOS-6018 STEREO
whatcha see is whatcha get
Featuring
IN THE RAIN
the dramatics

PR 10004

PRESTIGE STEREO

NO WAY!
BOOGALOO JOE JONES
GROVER WASHINGTON JR. / SONNY PHILLIPS / BUTCH CORNELL / JIMMY LEWIS / BERNARD PURDIE

DESIGN/PHOTO: DON SCHLITTEN

SOUL MAKOSSA
AFRIQUE

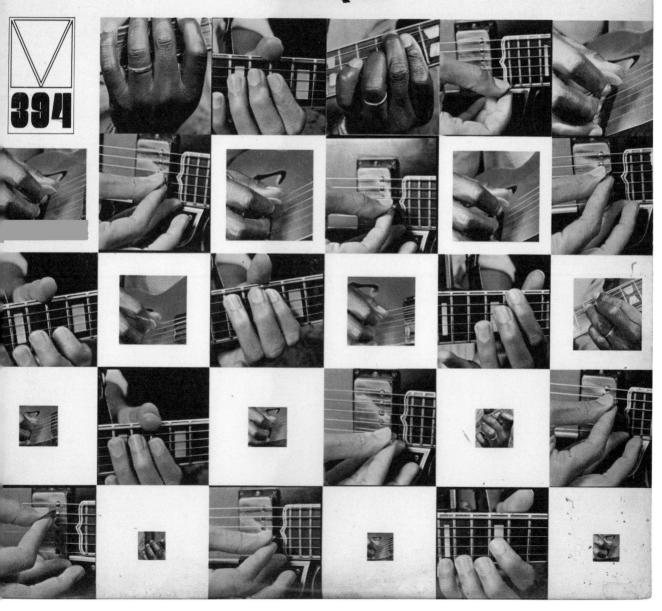

LA LUPE
ES LA REINA
LA LUPE
THE QUEEN

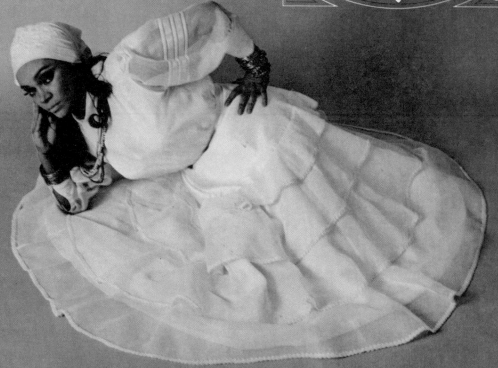

TICO
HIGH FIDELITY

A DIVISION OF ROULETTE RECORDS INC.

LP-1192

STEREO COMPATIBLE DAP-004

NATURALLY

SHARON JONES
AND THE DAP-KINGS

ARETHA
live at fillmore west

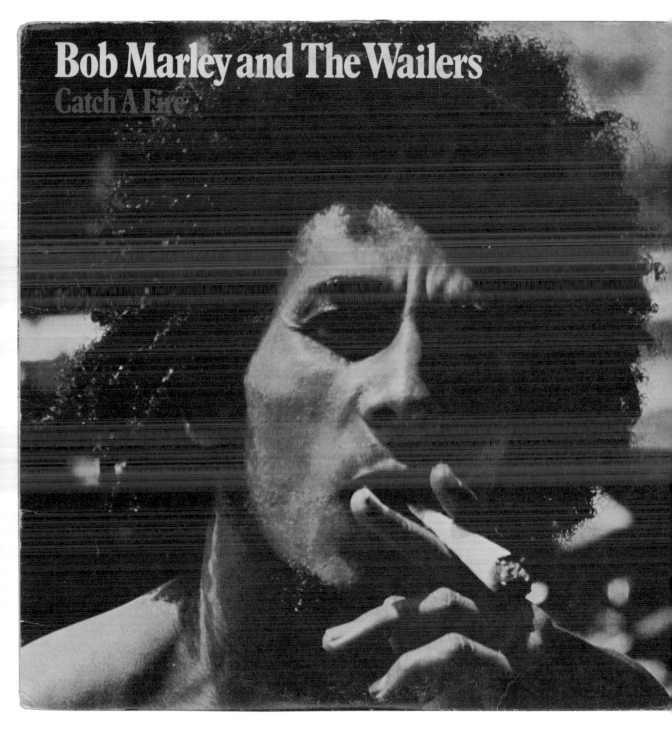

GM 3305/STEREO
GEORGE FREEMAN
MAN & WOMAN
GM 3305 GEORGE FREEMAN/MAN & WOMAN

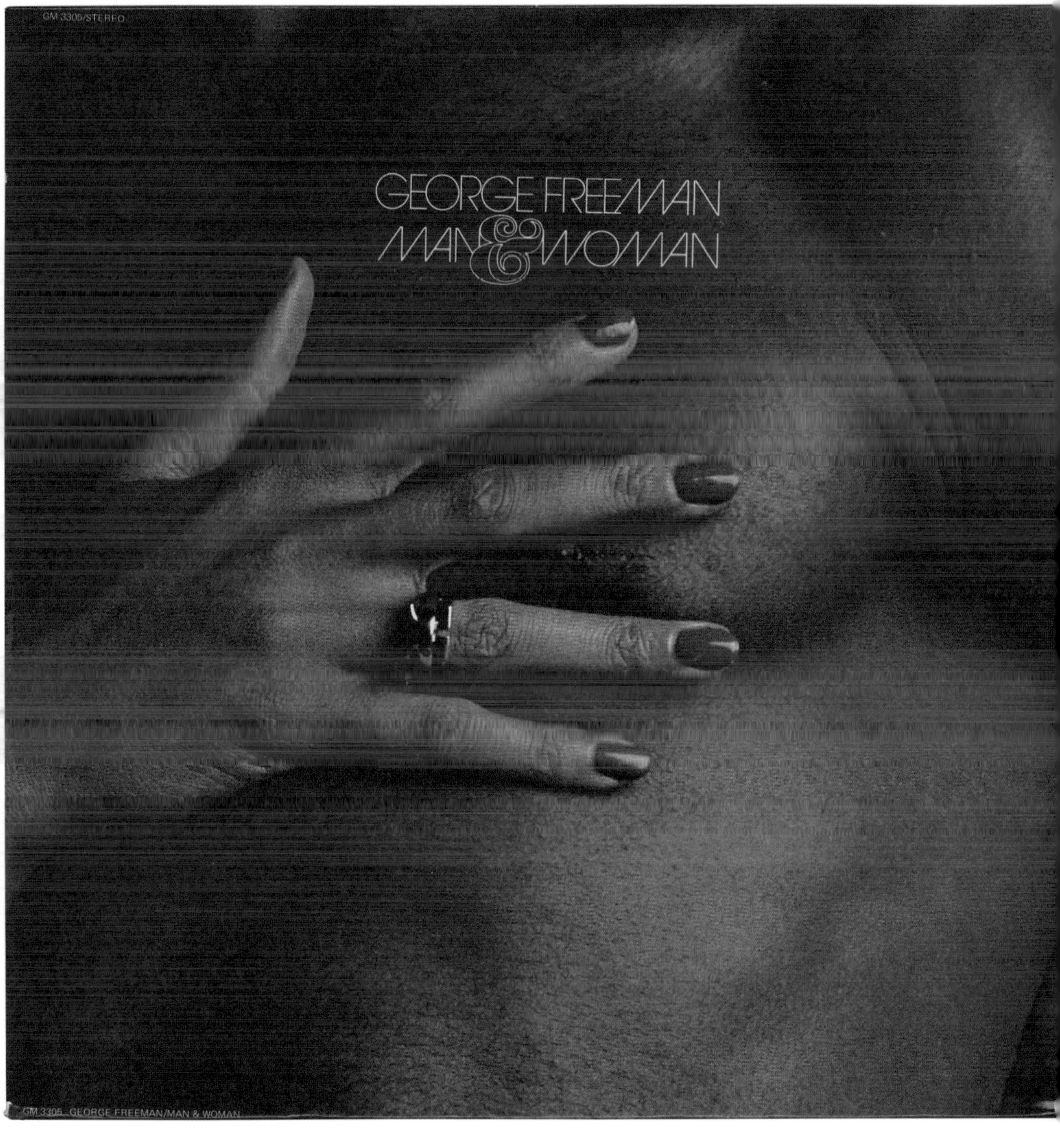

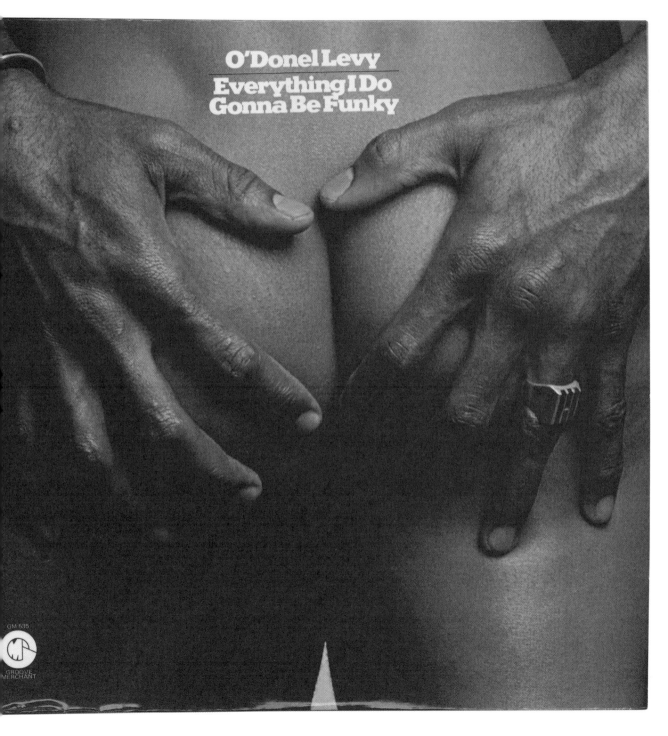

Terry Reid : River

SD 725

Sonambient

HORDE CATALYTIQUE POUR LA FIN

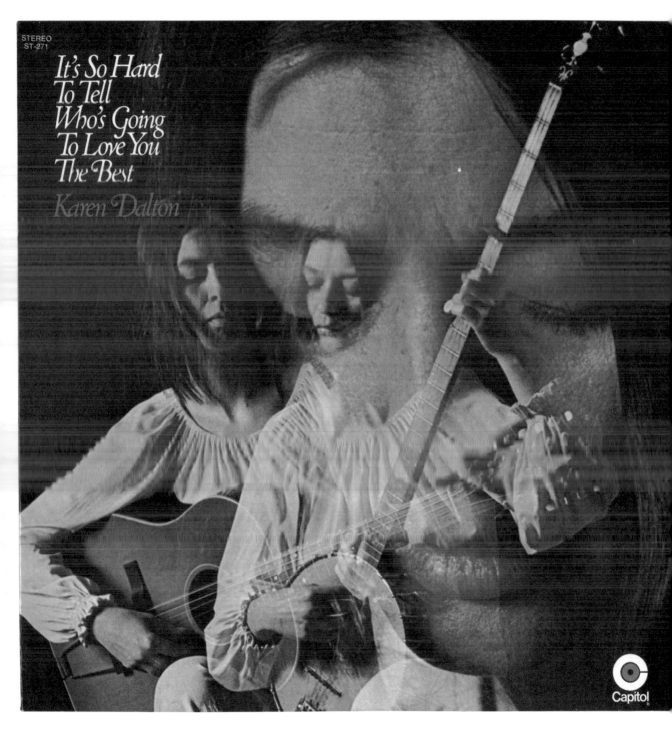

CAT

711

Black Knight

LSP-3846 STEREO

THE PRIVATE SEA OF DREAMS

GRUPPO

RCA VICTOR
DYNAGROOVE
RECORDING

IMPROVISATIONS
MOOD MUSIC FOR
MODERN DREAM
INTENSIONS

DENNIS OLIVIERI  COME TO THE PARTY

PROMOTION - Not For Sale

Oracle Records
1083

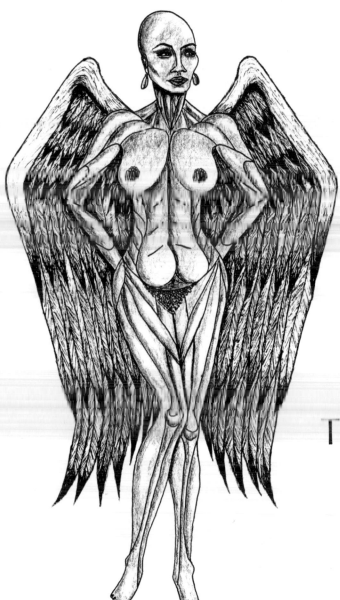

THE
PARIS SMITH
QUINTET

THOUGHT SEEDS

SOUND COMMUNICATION BY THE BOTTLENOSED DOLPHIN

JKC
1978

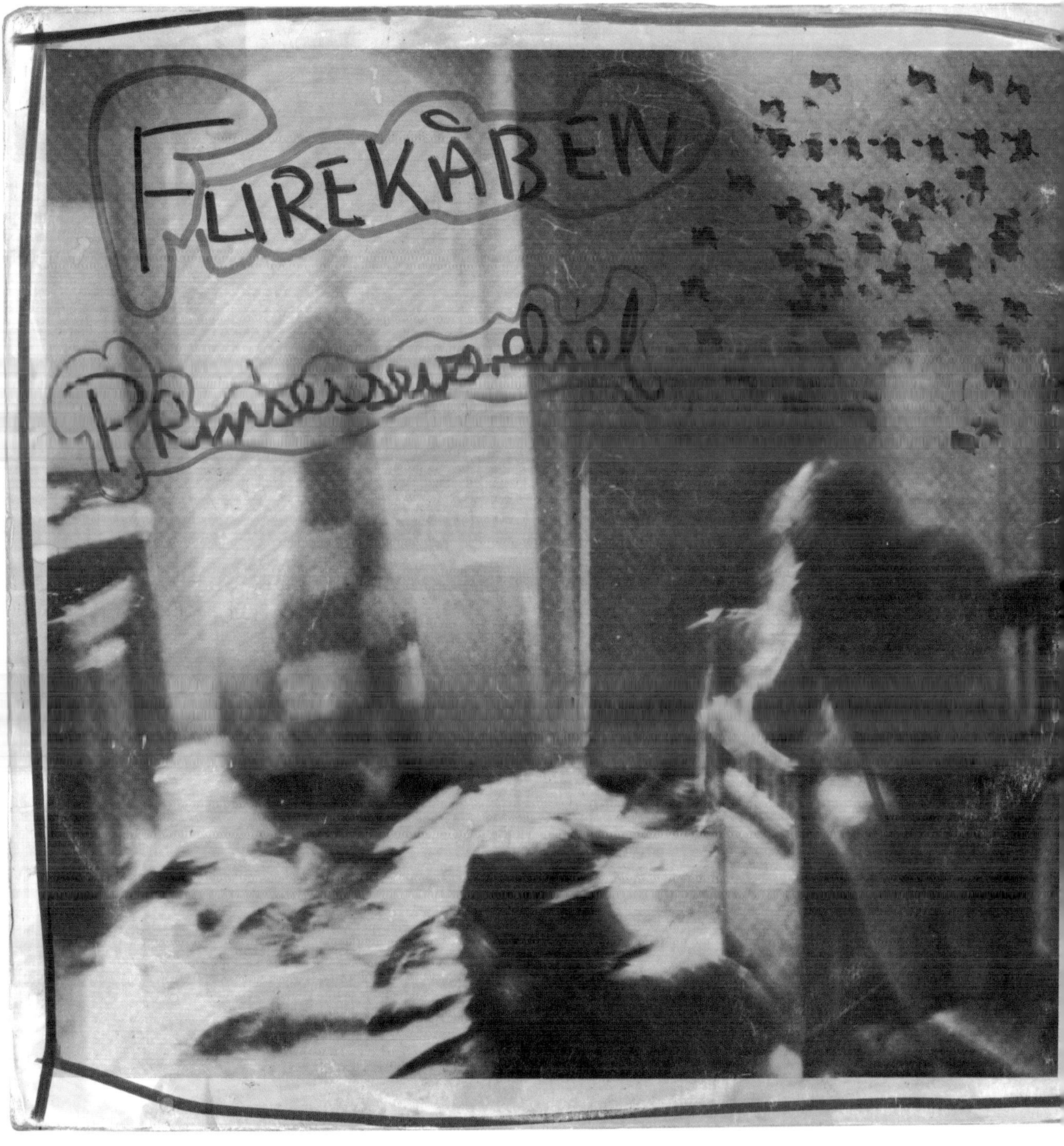
FLUREKÂBEN

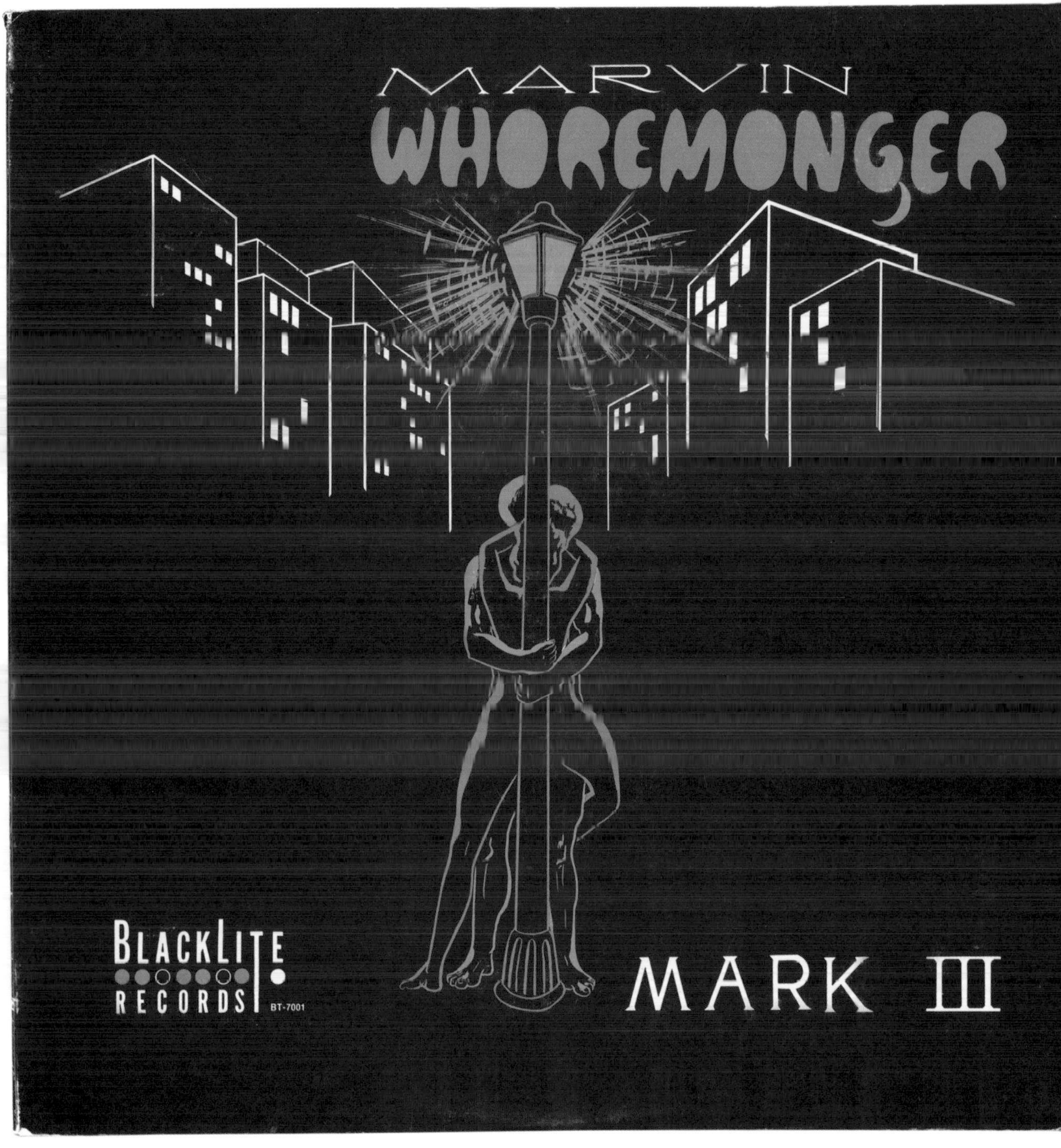
MARVIN
WHOREMONGER
BLACKLITE
RECORDS
BT-7001
MARK III

Cover Story 07

STEREO 214
VOL.1
sparrow's
troubadours
hot &
sweet
ROW'S TROUBADOURS • HOT & SWEET •

Mambo
For CATS
RCA VICTOR
LPM-1063
A "NEW ORTHOPHONIC" HIGH FIDELITY RECORDING
© RCA Printed in U. S. A.

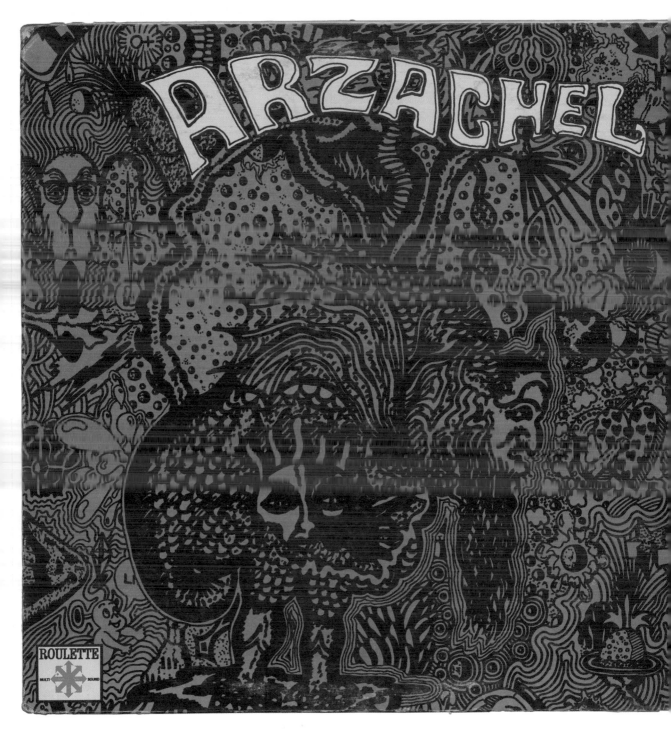

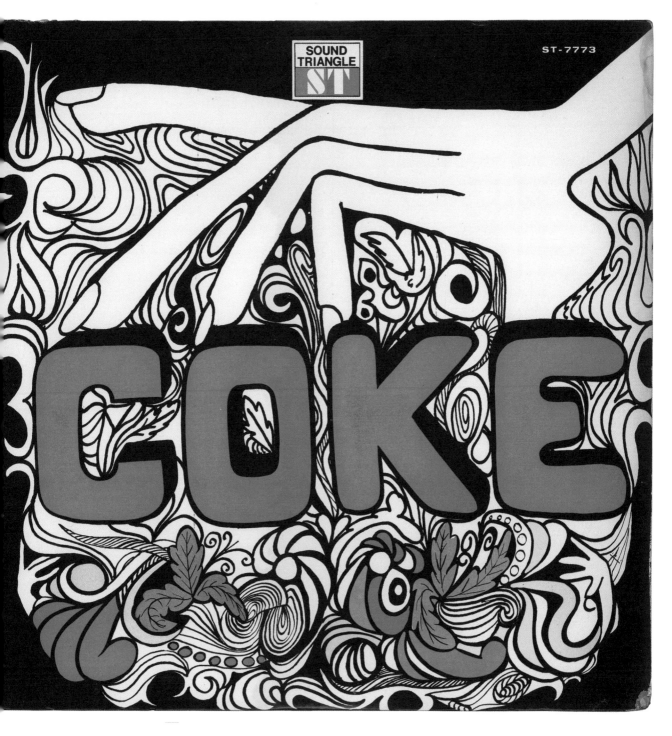

AV-11005- STEREO

chakachas

◢◢AVCO

BREAK DANCE
ELECTRIC BOOGIE
WEST STREET MOB

SUGARHILL RECORDS LTD.

SH 9201

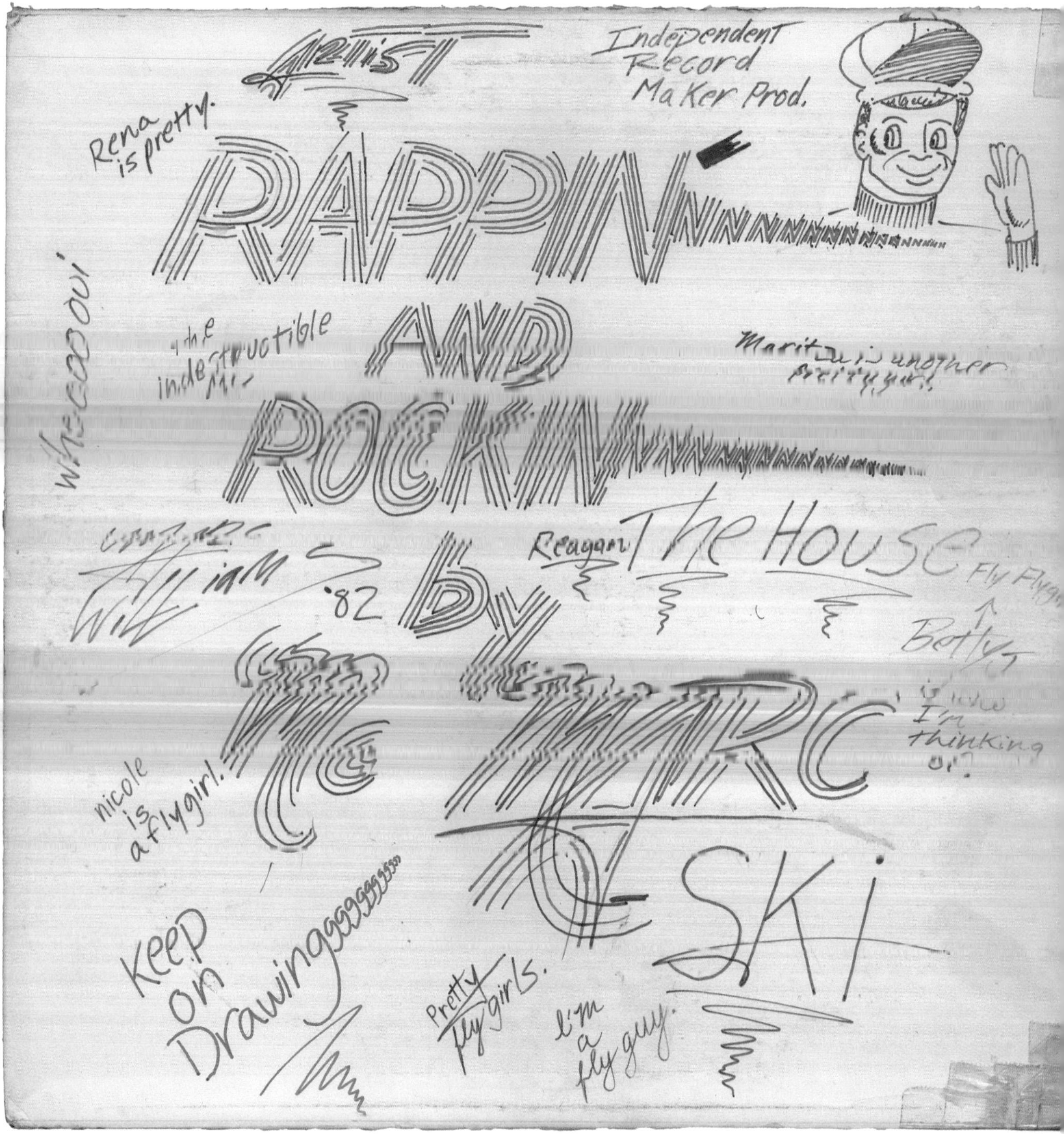

ARTIST

Independent Record Maker Prod.

Rena is pretty.

RAPPIN'

wheeeooui'

the indestructible Mr.

AND

Marita is another prettyyy!

ROCKIN'

Williams '82 by

Reagan

The HOUSE

Fly Fly...

Botty T

nicole is a flygirl.

MC MARC

I'm thinking of.

SKI

KEEP on Drawinggggggg

Pretty fly girls.

i'm a fly guy.

I Fell In L♥ve With a Prostitute

Sermon by:

Rev. Jasper Williams

Church Door
LP 1001

Gut Holz!

Stiftungsfest
im
Kegelklub

Die Schwestern und Brüder
vom Kegelklub
„RATZE 09"
und der Musikverein
„SAUSE"

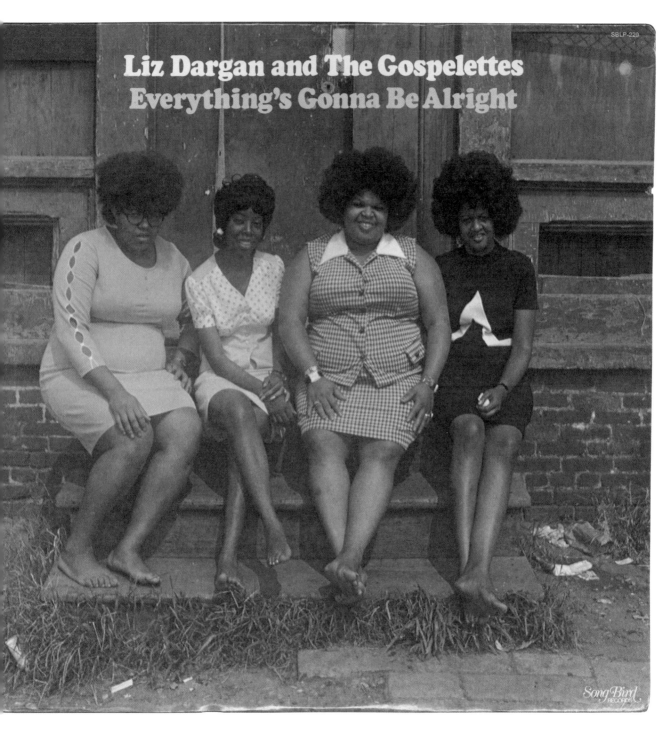

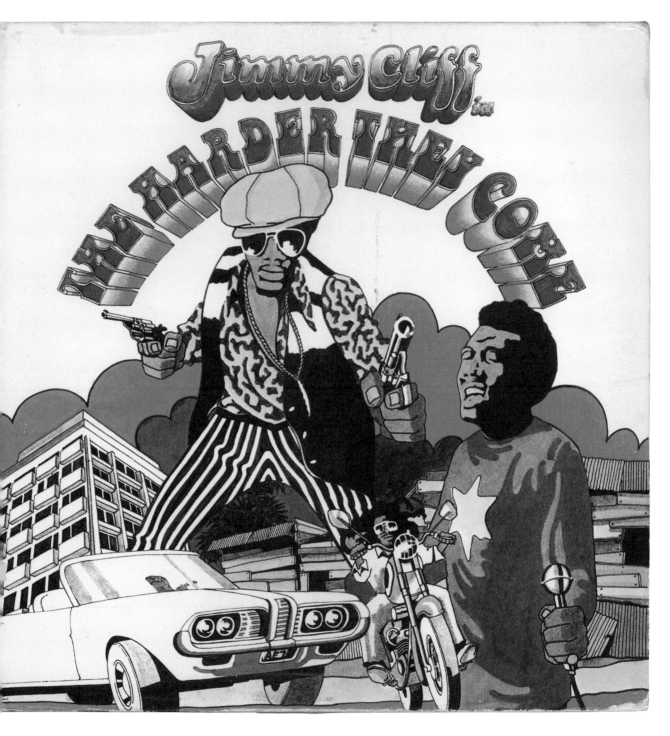

Where my HEAD is at

TITO RAMOS

cotique

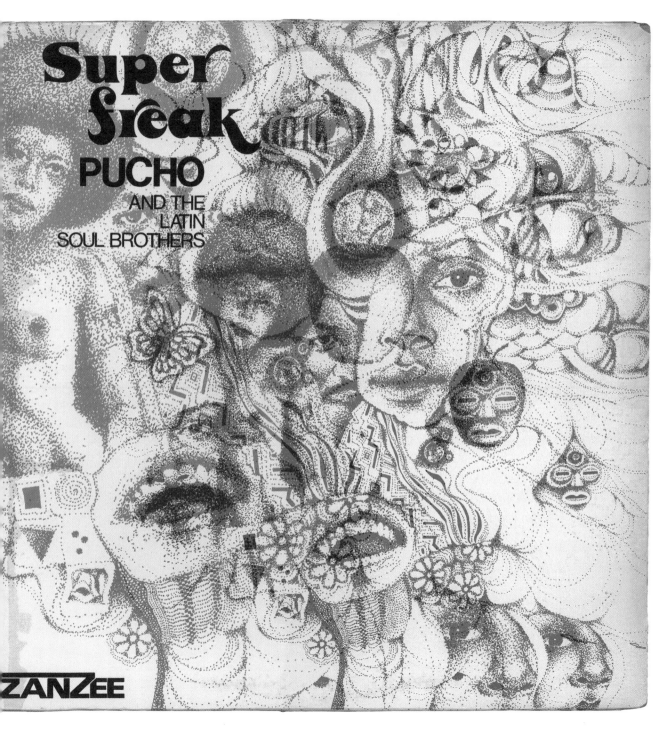

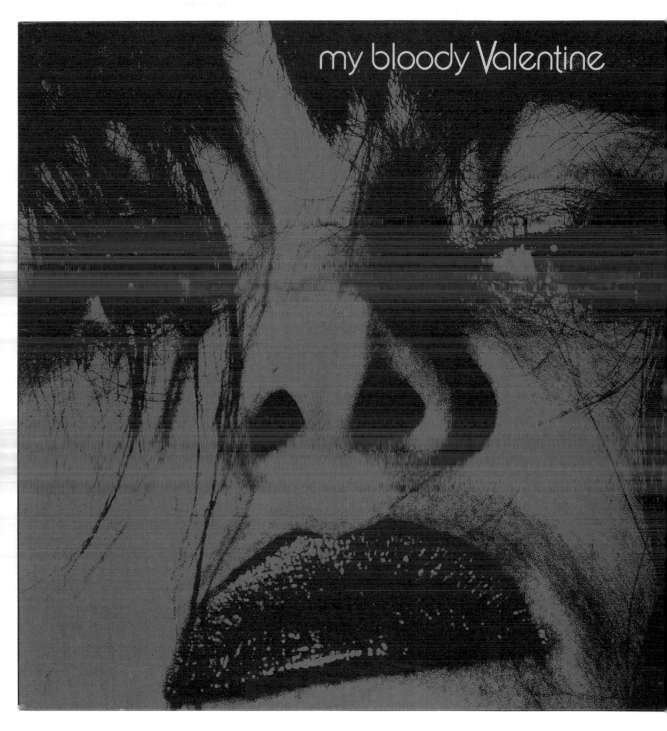

GAINSBOURG LOVE ON THE BEAT

MVS-53
Series 0698
Compatible Stereo

MONGO SANTAMARIA
SOFRITO

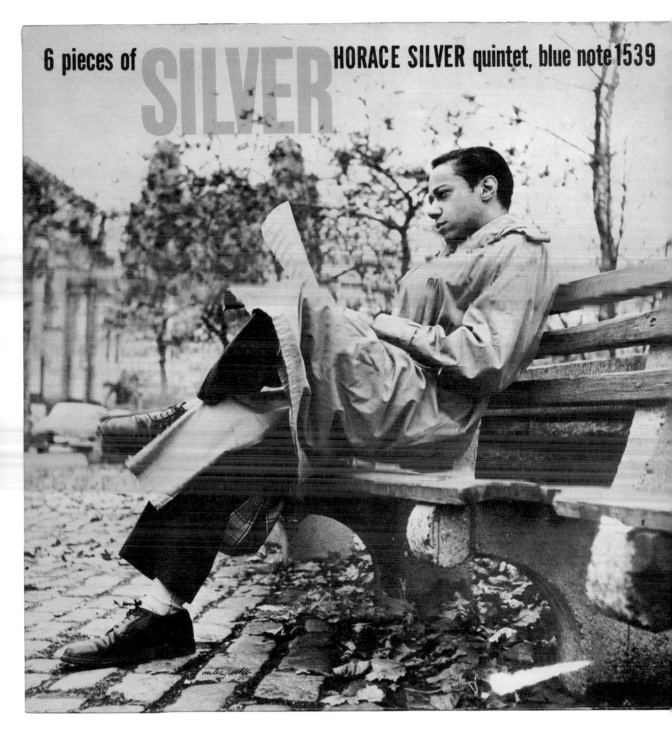

BLUE NOTE 1562

the stylings of
SILVER

"saturday night special"

The Lyman Woodard Organization

STRATA
RECORDS

GO WITH
THE FLOW

MICHAEL WHITE'S
MAGIC MUSIC
COMPANY

impulse

STRING BEAT

Muza
POLSKIE NAGRANIA
SX 1276

ORKIESTRA
PR i TV W ŁODZI
DYRYGUJE
HENRYK DEBICH

Flisak

SPLASH

Volume 2
Blue Note 1552

JIMMY SMITH AT THE ORGAN

with Lou Donaldson
Kenny Burrell
Eddie McFadden
Art Blakey
Donald Bailey

ROOT DOWN
JIMMY SMITH LIVE!

8806

Verve

COMPATIBLE
stereo
SERIES 0598
SERIES 0598
"I can see"
RALFI PAGAN
FANIA

LEON WARE
MUSICAL MASSAGE

TODAY AND TOMORROW
McCOY TYNER

STEREO Impulse! A-63

McCOY TYNER TRIO
WITH ROY HAYNES AND HENRY GRIMES
REACHING FOURTH

impulse!
STEREO A-33

JORGE DALTO "CHEVERE"

01

02

03

04

05

06

07

08

Cover Story 09

10

11

12

SH 9124
The Treacherous Three
SugarHill
SUGARHILL RECORDS LTD

ATOMIC Bomb

NEW PROCESS
CSG STEREO
COMPATIBLE

ROLAND KIRK
the inflated tear

ATLANTIC

SC 1502

DIRAM   LDR 2001

Sonny Sonny **CITY BOYS**
BAND

led by

Ɔheaba J. A. Adofo
THE BLACK CHINESE

NYA
ASEM
HWE

SIDE ONE
1. NYA ASEM HWE (Highlife)
2. ƆSƆ NNGYA M'AKYIR (Reggae)
3. DWEN A MEPE (Mid. Tem)
4. ƆBE NIPA SEE WO A (Highlife)

SIDE TWO
1. AKUTIABO (Adowa)
2. ƆNKWANOMA DEDE (Highlife)
3. BAABI DUHYEE (Odonson)
4. NKO BESIE (Highlife)

HIGHER PLANE BREEZE

OFEGE

STEREO
POLP
015

STEREO

JOHNNY ADAMS

heart & soul

GEORGIA MORNING DEW
IN A MOMENT OF WEAKNESS
REAL LIVE LIVING HURTIN' MAN
LONELY MAN
I WON'T CRY
RELEASE ME
PROUD WOMAN
I CAN'T BE ALL BAD
A LOSING BATTLE
LIVING ON YOUR LOVE
RECONSIDER ME

international
records
SSS #5

JOE BATAAN

"Mr. New York And The East Side Kids"

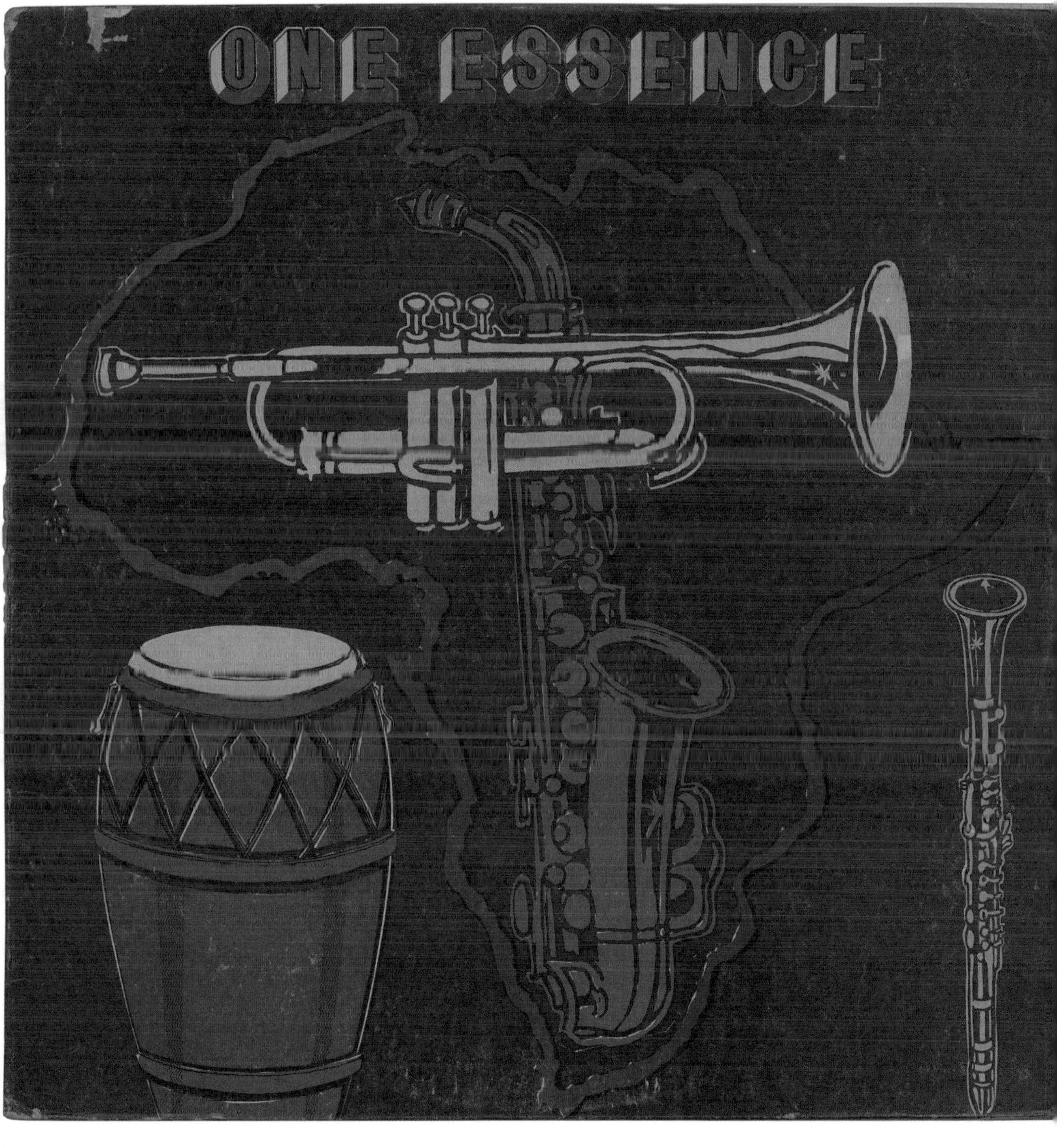
ONE ESSENCE

SIMMER DOWN..
SURVIVAL
From
A DEPARTMENT OF
FEMI EWETADE
PROMOTIONS
Leventis STORES
MARINA
1st floor
Wishing you happy listening
ALLEN ROAD,

The Boys

Sex Symbols

·:o: simbolos sexuales :o:·

COTIQUE

MONO C-1038

AmorBuenosAires

JORGE LOPEZ RUIZ

CATALYST
CAT-7908

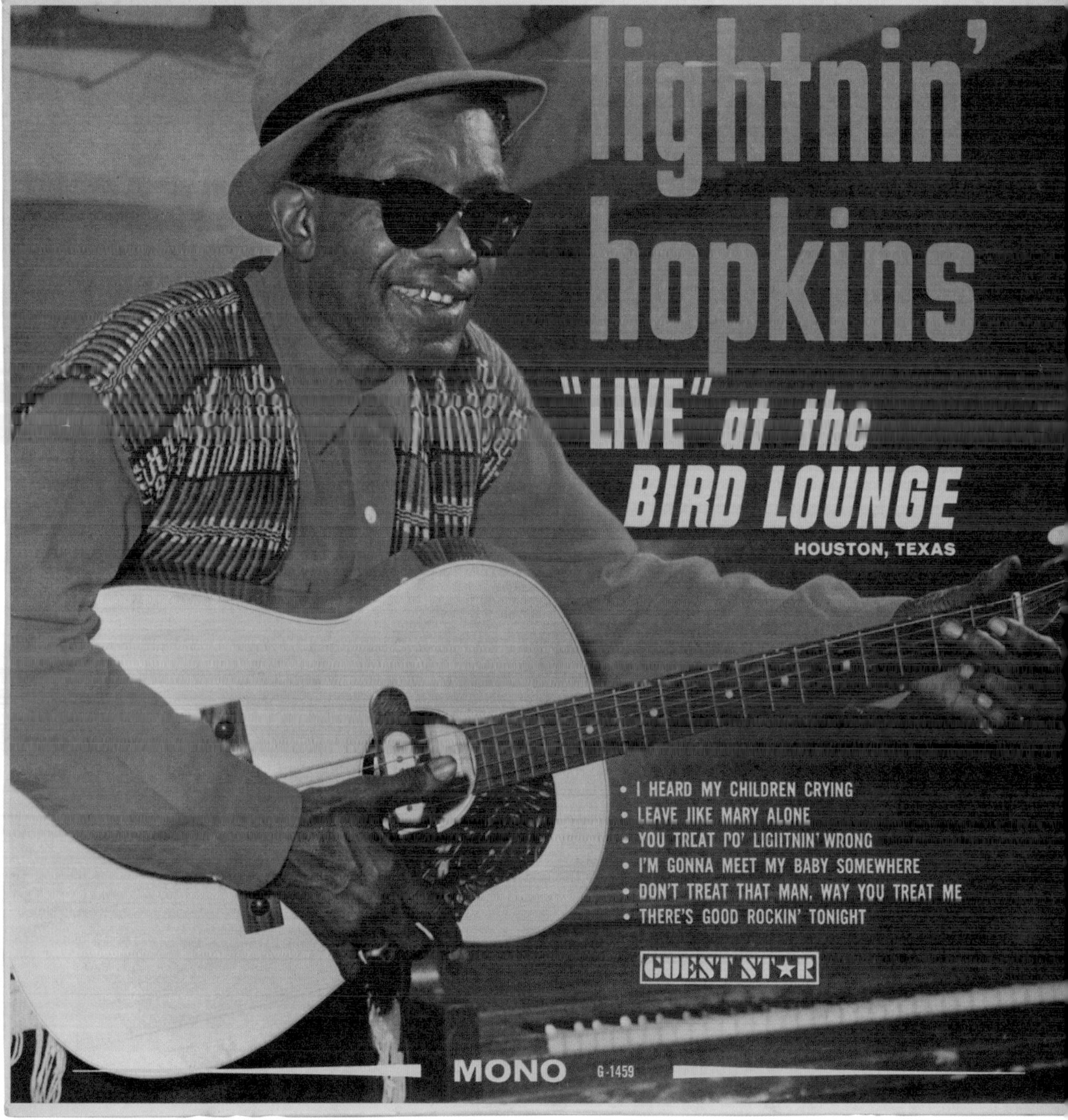
lightnin' hopkins
"LIVE" at the BIRD LOUNGE
HOUSTON, TEXAS
• I HEARD MY CHILDREN CRYING
• LEAVE JIKE MARY ALONE
• YOU TREAT PO' LIGHTNIN' WRONG
• I'M GONNA MEET MY BABY SOMEWHERE
• DON'T TREAT THAT MAN, WAY YOU TREAT ME
• THERE'S GOOD ROCKIN' TONIGHT
GUEST STAR
MONO
G-1459

DJINNS MUSIC

DISCOGRAM

exode rural

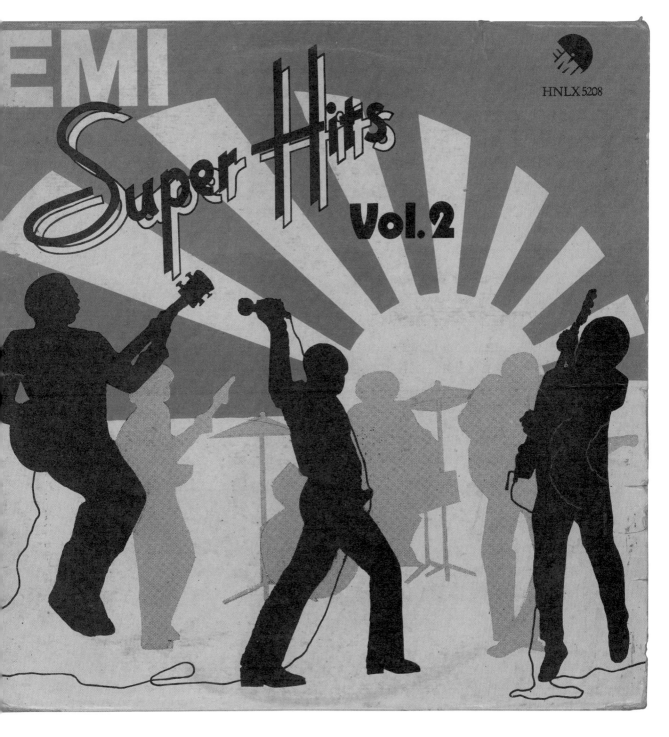

Miss Butters

RCA VICTOR
DYNAGROOVE
RECORDING

the family tree

LPM-3955

01

02

03

04

05

06

07

08

09

Cover Story 10

11

12

STEREO

P&B 7120

HEY WORLD!

Sir William Portis, Jr.

THE ELEMENTS OF SOUND

'Sabdu'

Rick

'Blodeé'

Jonnie

Danny

BY THE TIME I GET TO PHOENIX

HAND CLAPPIN' MUSIC

U. S. ATLANTIC FLEET NAVY SHOW BAND

HOTTER THAN HELL

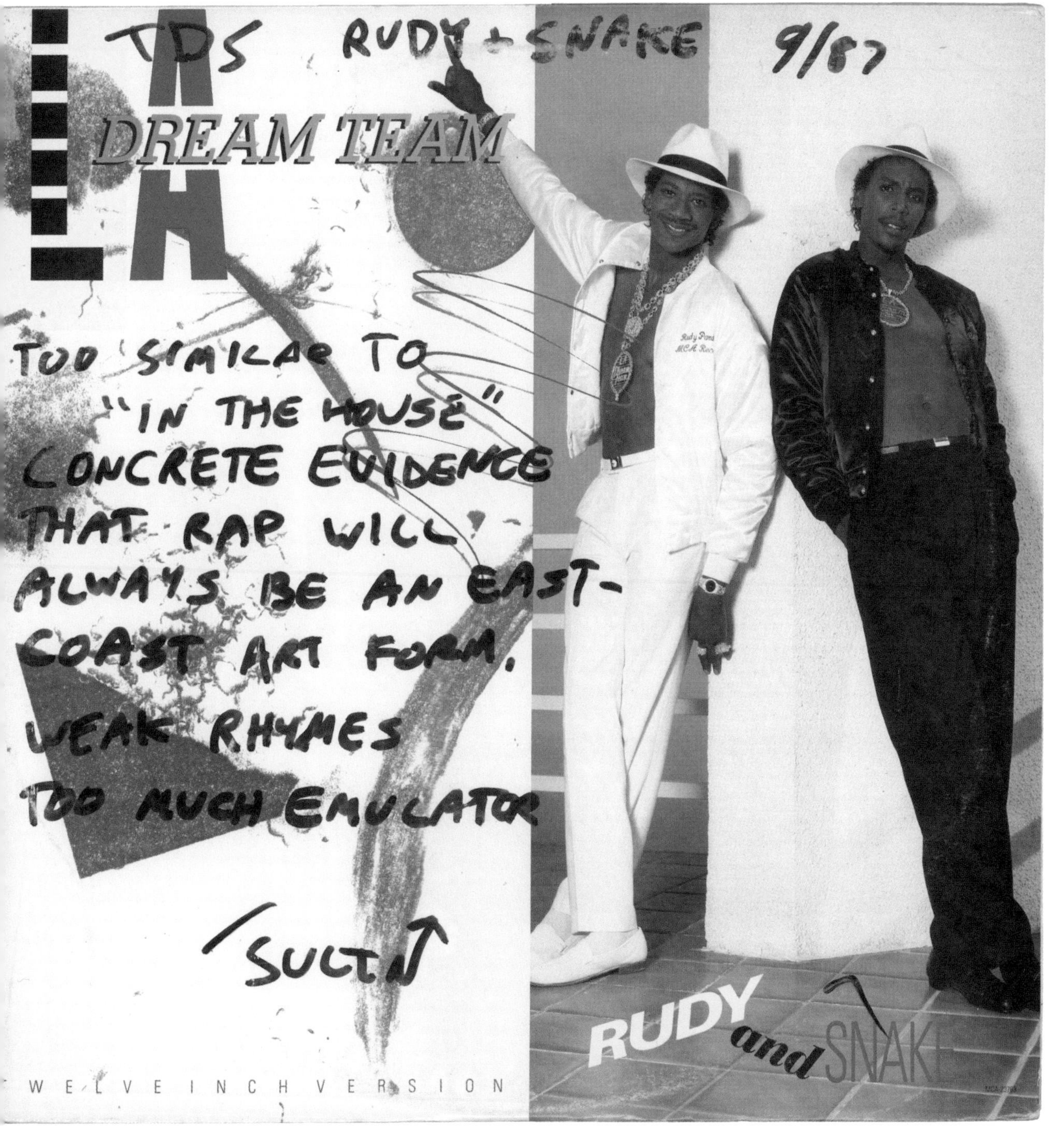

TDS RUDY + SNAKE 9/87

L.A. DREAM TEAM

TOO SIMILAR TO
"IN THE HOUSE"
CONCRETE EVIDENCE
THAT RAP WILL
ALWAYS BE AN EAST-
COAST ART FORM.
WEAK RHYMES
TOO MUCH EMULATOR

/SULTN↑

RUDY and SNAKE

WELVE INCH VERSION

DADISI KOMOLAFE

NS-3035

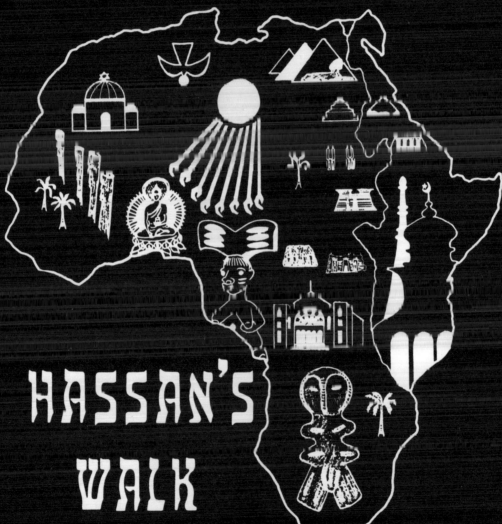

HASSAN'S WALK

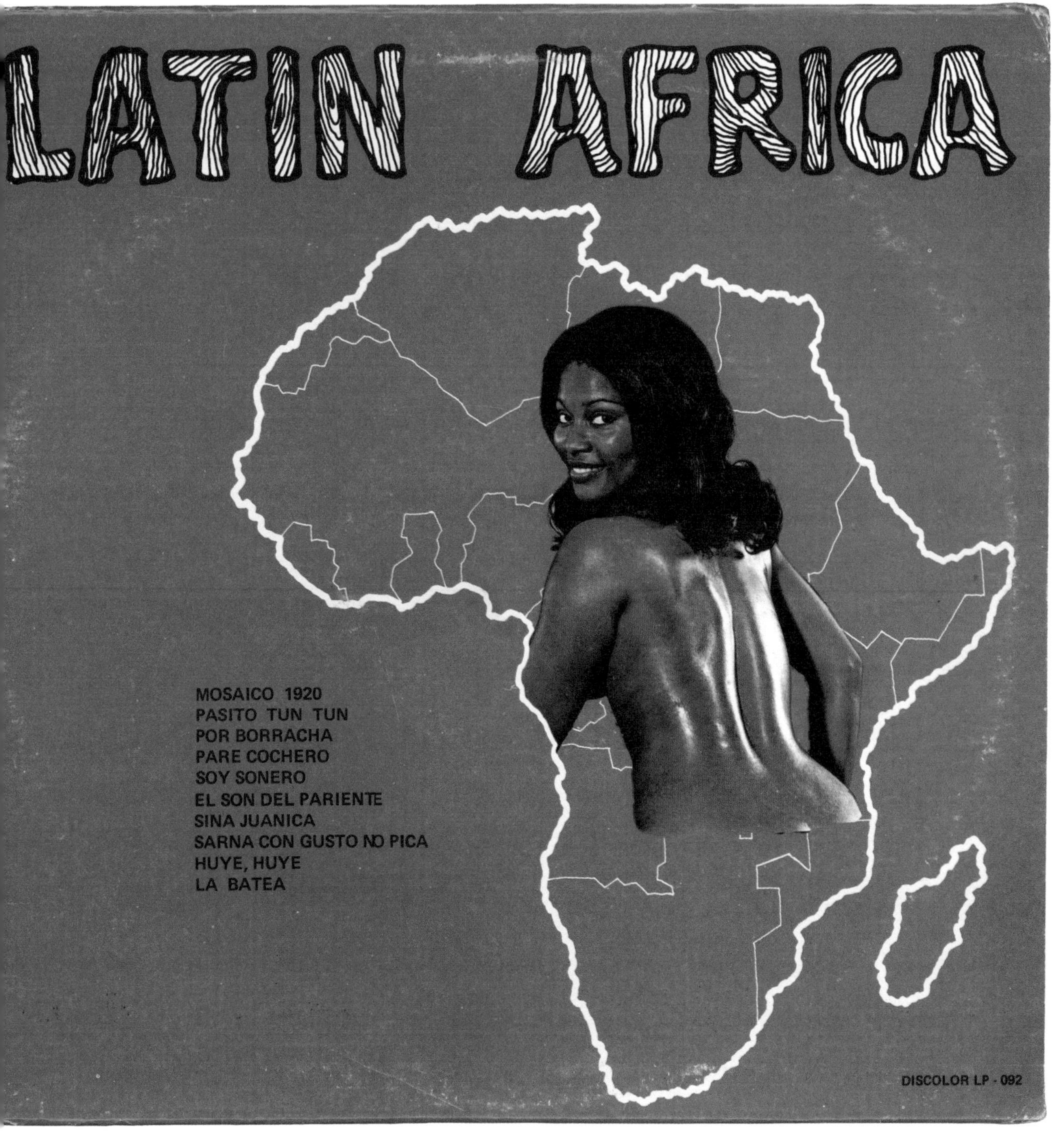

LATIN AFRICA

MOSAICO 1920
PASITO TUN TUN
POR BORRACHA
PARE COCHERO
SOY SONERO
EL SON DEL PARIENTE
SINA JUANICA
SARNA CON GUSTO NO PICA
HUYE, HUYE
LA BATEA

DISCOLOR LP - 092

THE NEW LAMONT DOZIER ALBUM   LOVE AND BEAUT

INVICTUS
RECORDS

INVICTUS STEREO

KZ 33134

the
GOOD

the
BAD,

the
UGLY

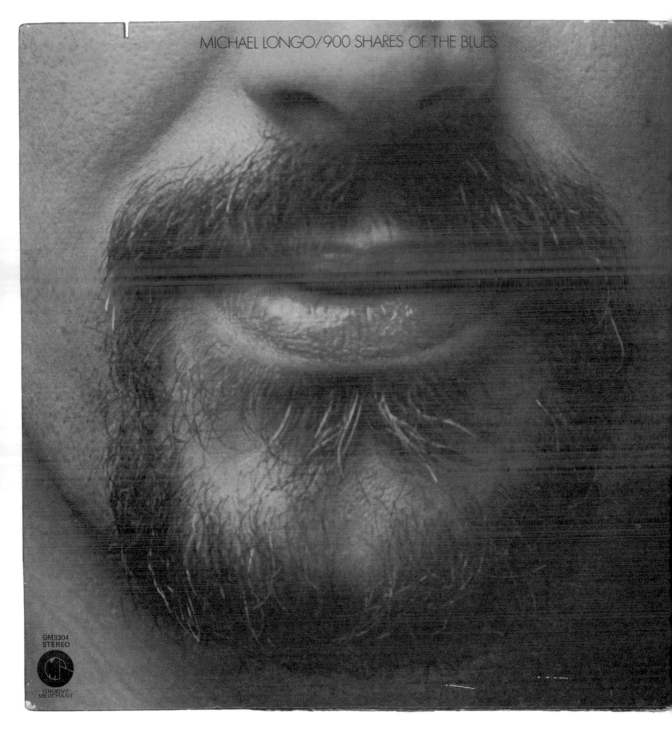

MICHAEL LONGO/900 SHARES OF THE BLUES.

GM3304
STEREO

GROOVE
MERCHANT

El Bigote

STEREO
SOUND TRIANGLE
ST
STS-8000

Luis Santi
y su conjunto

PARTY PEOPLE

Rappermatical 5
The brake is death

PEP 1002

REMIXED & REMASTERED

ORIGINAL MIX

One Side

Other Side

STEREO
JOSIE 4011

JOSIE

LOOK–KA PY PY

THE   METERS

DUMP NIXON

George McGovern For President

McGOVERN/SHRIVER

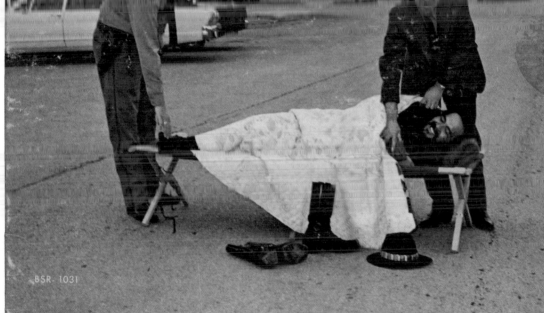

BIG LU y VALEN y
LOS MUCHACHOS

STEREO

BSR- 1031

UN AMIGO BORRACHO

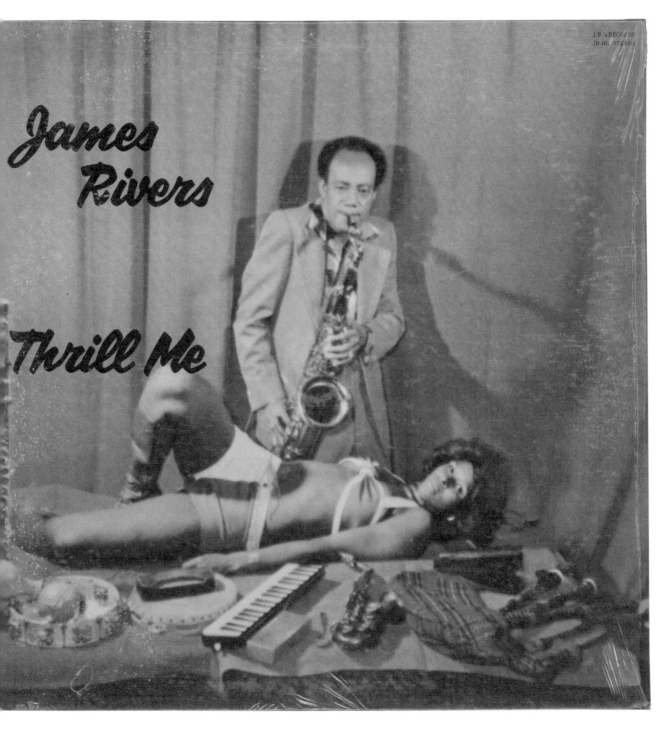

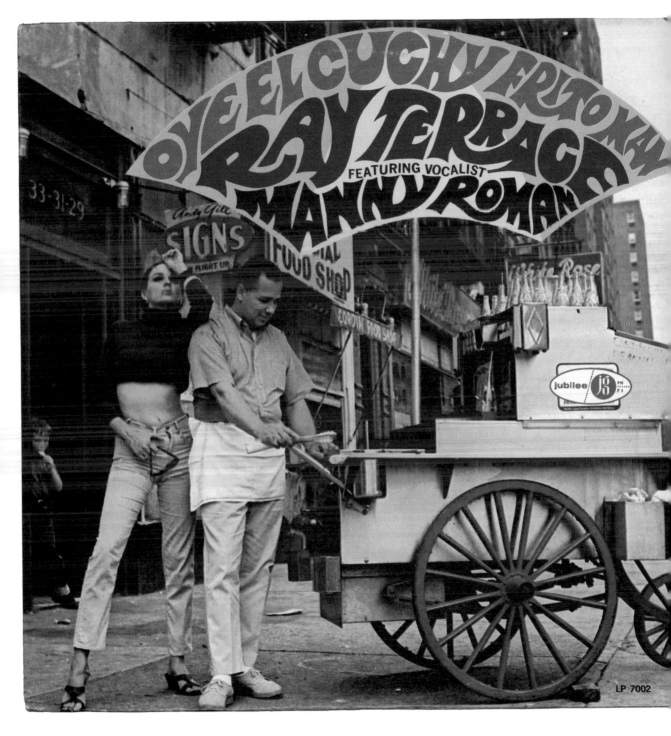

EL SONIDO MODERNO DE
THE MODERN SOUNDS OF
AL ESCOBAR
Two Guys
TICO
HIGH FIDELITY
AL ESCOBAR
and His Orchestr
LP 1184

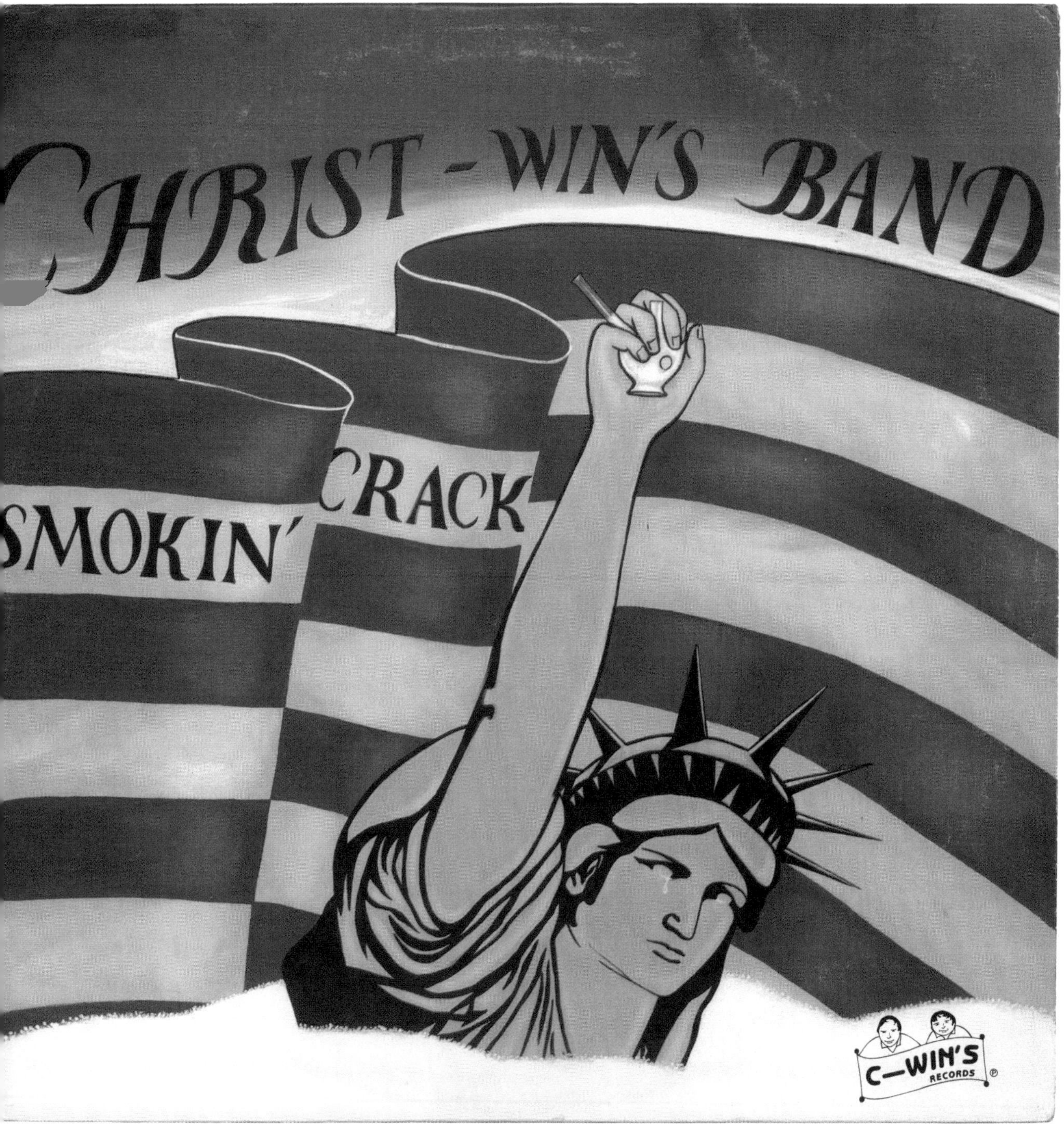
CHRIST-WIN'S BAND
SMOKIN'
CRACK
C—WIN'S
RECORDS

LIONEL HAMPTON

OFF INTO A BLACK THING

BL 7-54213

Brunswick
RECORDS

POETRY:

THE BLACK VOICES:
ON THE STREET IN WATTS

stereo

ALX 1970 STEREO

CHUCK BROWN AND THE SOUL SEARCHERS BUSTIN' LOOS

SOR-3076

O Be RECORDS
STEREO

Kawaida

NINA SIMONE

UP FRONT

UPF 145

The Afro-Eurasian Eclipse

A Suite in Eight Parts

Duke Ellington

Fantasy F 9498

STEREO GM 503

GROOVE MERCHANT

JIMMY McGRIFF

GROOVE
GREASE

Shakara

EMI ∙ TEMPSA

ELD 02.21.213 (STEREO)

FELA and THE AFRICA 70

A FILM OF MELVIN VAN PEEBLES THE ORIGINAL CAST SOUNDTRACK ALBUM

STAX RECORDS STEREO STS-300

SWEET SWEETBACK'S
BAADASSSSS SONG

S 5129 STEREO

The Black Motion Picture Experience

SUPER FLY ★ SHAFT
TROUBLE MAN ★ ACROSS 110TH ST
SLAUGHTER
FREDDIE'S DEAD
LADY SINGS THE BLUES
BEN ★ 2001

The Cecil Holmes Soulful Sounds

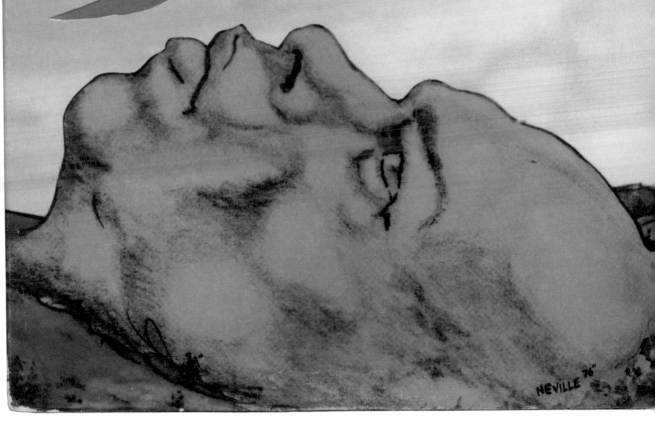

P-66002 TWO-RECORD SET

CHARLES EARLAND

LEAVING THIS PLANET

FREDDIE HUBBARD
JOE HENDERSON

Prestige

CYS 1312
CAYTRONICS

STEREO
Playable on
Monaural Equipment

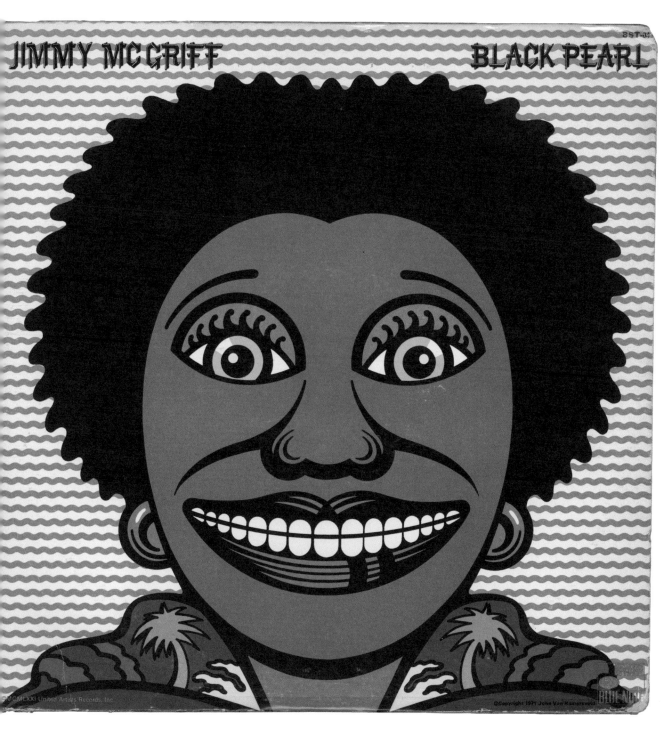

PORT AUTHORITY

IRA SULLIVAN

STRINGS ATTACHED

PR 7169

PA
USA

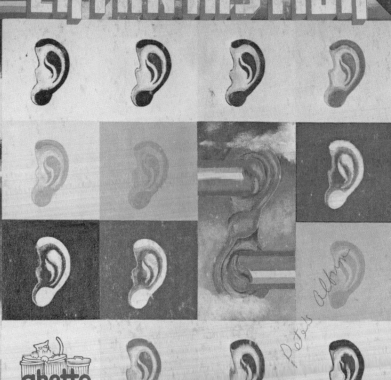

LA FANTASTICA

stereo 00

THE NAZTY
GOT TO MOVE
MANKIND
206
Space Boogie
Bicentennial
Rock & Roll
Within
Unlucky Love
No Deposit No Return
Maybe
Your Baby
I Need Love
Look
What
You've Done
It's
Summer
Time

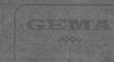

BTS 66

PAUL HUMPHREY
"America, Wake Up"

$1.98

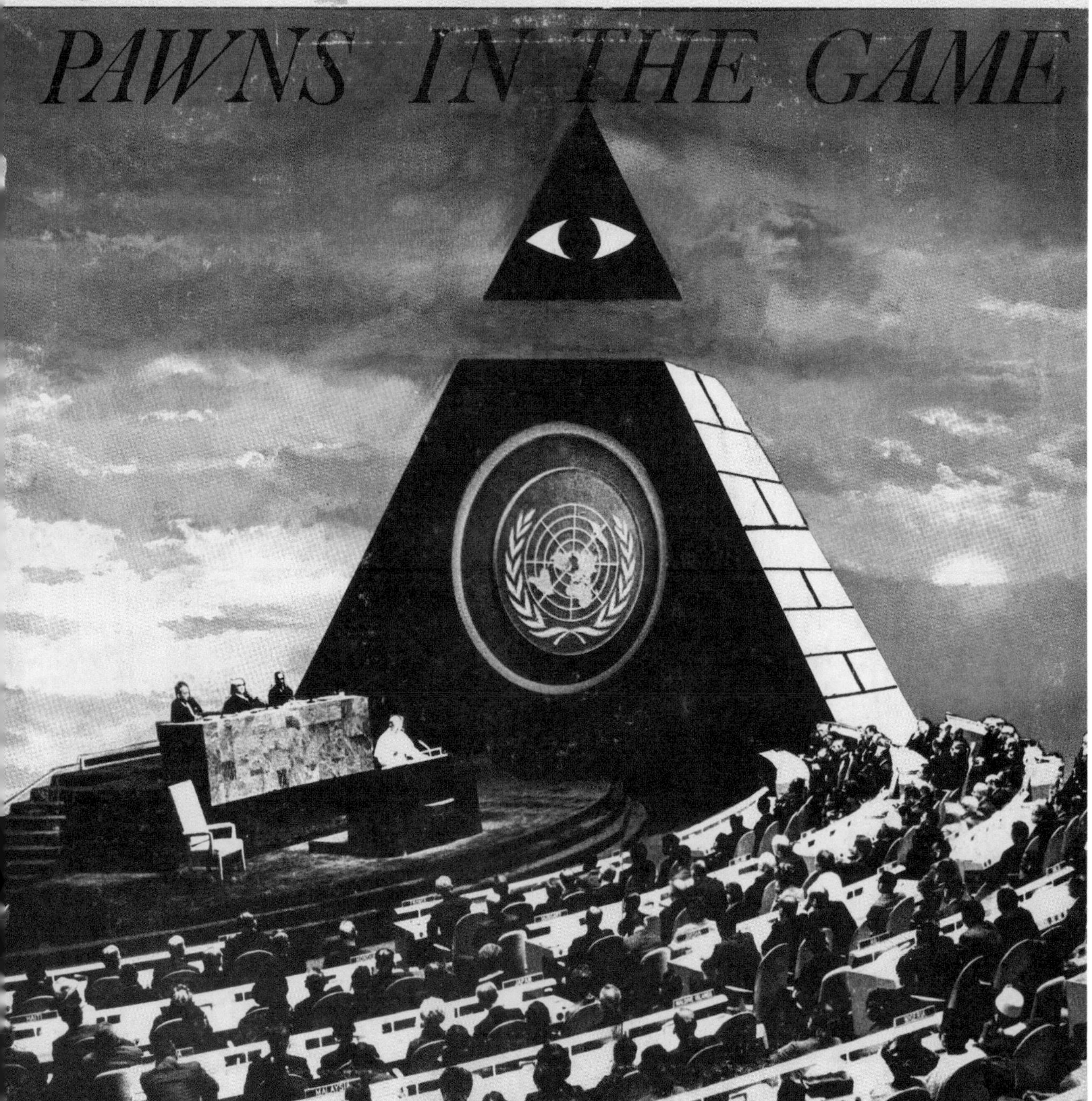
PAWNS IN THE GAME

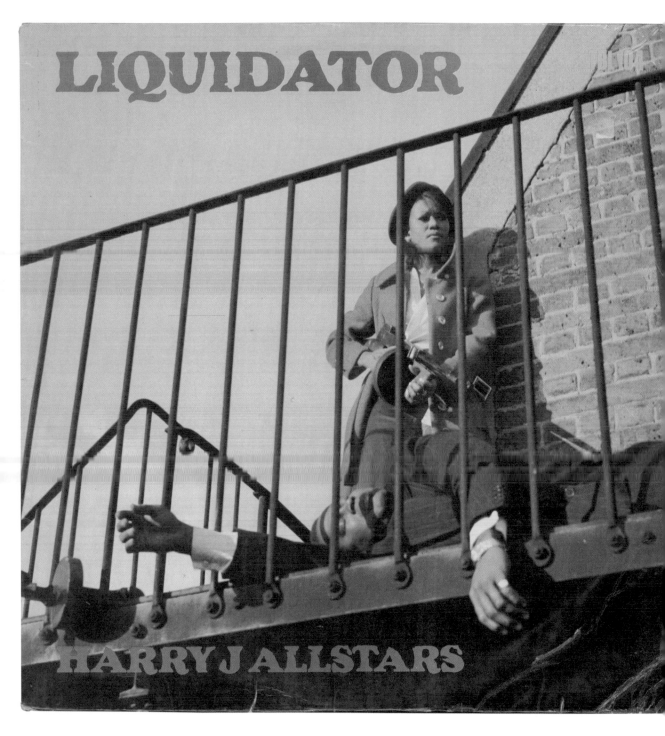

Live Recording in Long Kesh

SMASH
INTERNMENT
and
Injustice

PARA SUA
PROTEÇÃO

AP-1

አሊ : መሐመድ : በራ :

ALI MOHAMED BIRRA

big band '73 - the palo alto high school jazz ensemble

CFS-3198

THE ADMIRAL
DELE ABIODUN
AND HIS TOP HITTERS BAND

ADAWA SUPER SOUND

ADAWA SUPER SOUND

THE GUITAR AND THE GUN: A Collection of Ghanaian Highlife Dance Music.

NORDESTE:
Cordel, Repente, Canção

J. BORGES

STEREO • • LS 86014

LIMELIGHT

THE THREE SOUNDS

Printed in U.S.A. ©Wayne Printing Corp. 1965

THREE MOODS

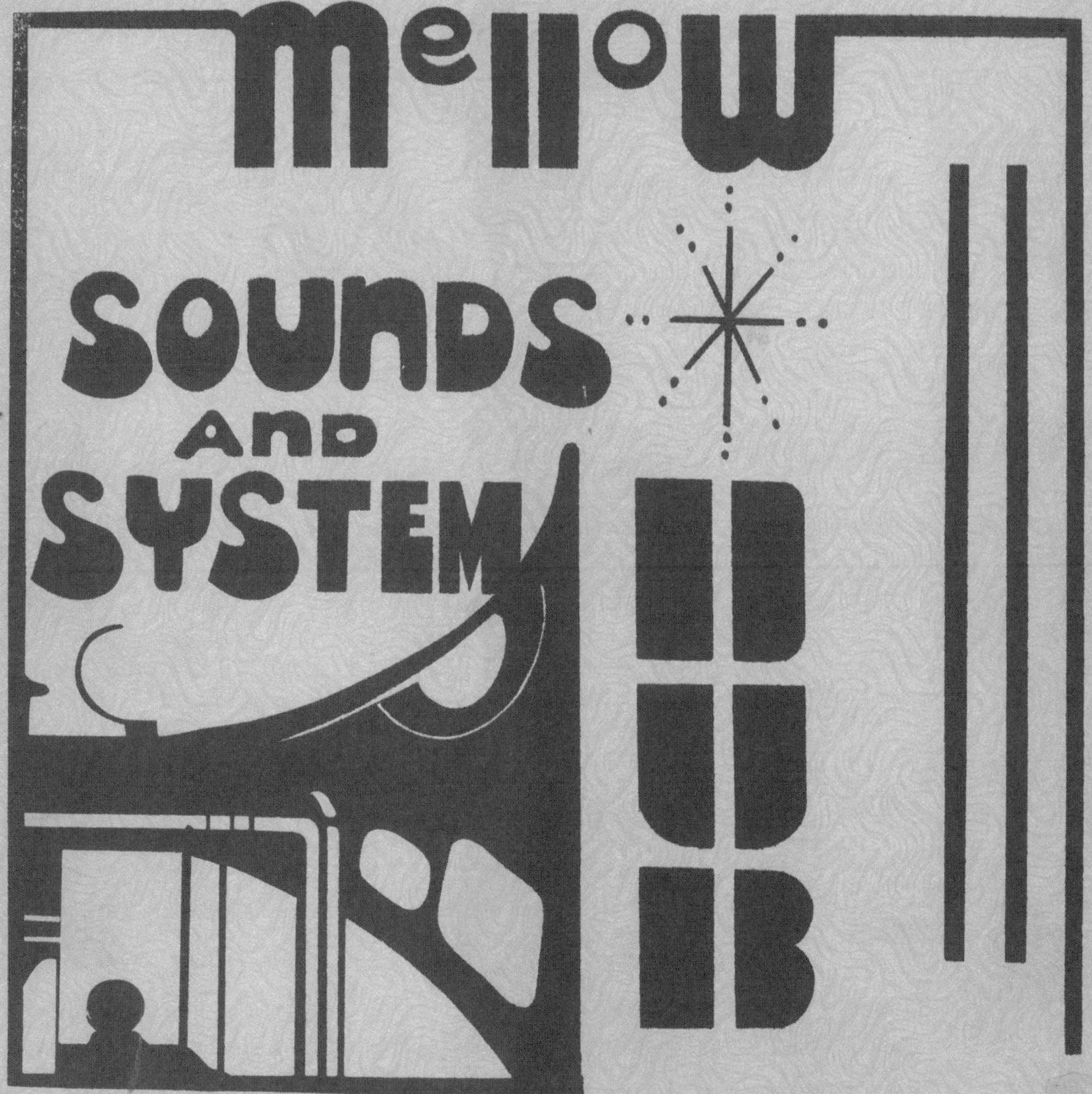
Mellow
SOUNDS
AND
SYSTEM
DUB

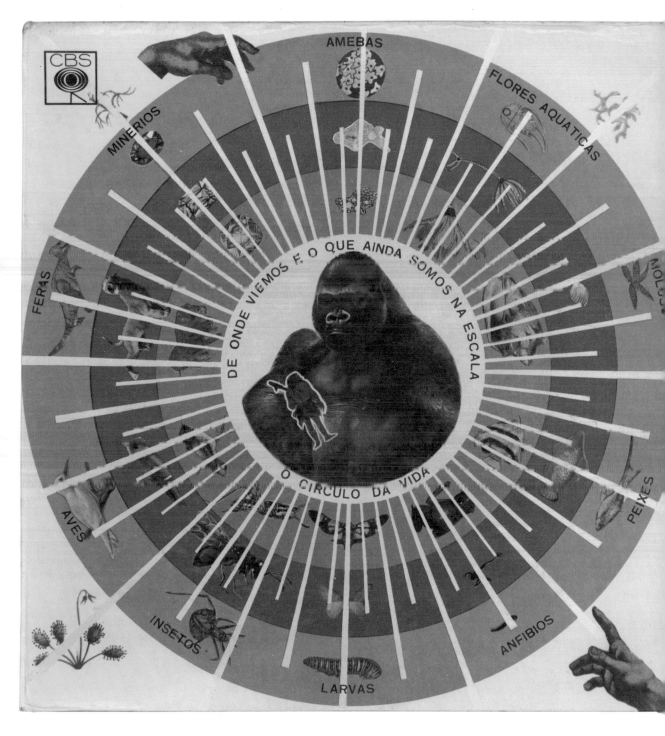

xingu

CANTOS E RITMOS

PHILIPS

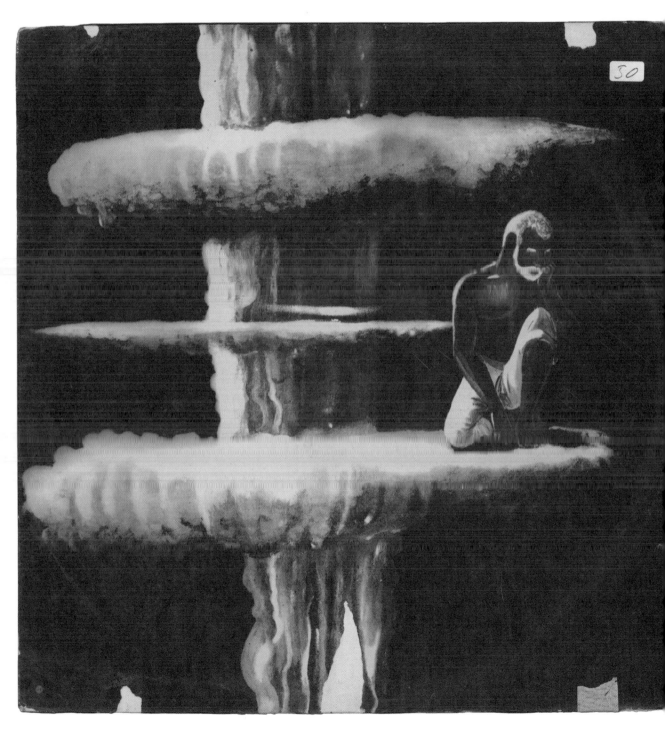

Discographies

COVER STORY 01 Dave Tompkins

01 **Burgess Meredith** *Burgess Meredith Reads Ray Bradbury* (Lively Arts LA30004) 1962
Design and photography: Don Schlitten

02 **Sleeping Bag Records** 12-inch sleeve

03 **Sir Mix-A-Lot** "I'm a Trip" (Nasty Mix Records IGU 6970) 1986
Art direction and design: Raymond Terada Design; photography and color tinting: Karen Moskowitz;
airbrushing: Al Doggett; color separations: Wescan; typesetting: the Type Gallery

04 **Real Raw** "Drop Them Drawers" (World Premiere Records RR-1000-1) 1989
Photography: Carl Perkins

05 **Freestyle** "Don't Stop the Rock" (Music Specialists Incorporated MSI-111) 1985
Art and design: M. Morell; art direction: Sweethack Clark On Tour; photography: Bob Lasky

06 **Gettovetts** *Missionaries Moving* (Island 90916-1) 1988
Photography and art direction: George DuDose; painting: Rammellzee

07 **Speakerhead** "The Adventures of Speakerhead" (Never Stop NS-1112) 1989

08 **Missy Mist** "Gettin' Bass" (Never Stop NS-1111) 1989

09 **LeJuan Love** *I Still Feel Good* (Skywalker Records XR104 A) 1989
Art and design: M. Morell; photography: Ed Robinson

10 **Lil' Mac** *The Lyrical Midget* (Yo Records YO-1231-ADJ) date unknown
Design: Steven Porter Graphic Design; photography: Kurt Coste

11 **Melted Men** *Rotten Hut Florist* (Nerve Rust Recordings) date unknown
Art direction: Erik Olofsen

12 **The Unknown DJ** "808 Beats" (Techno Hop Records THR-2) 1988
Artwork: Darryl "Lyrrad" Davis

13 **Oak Cliff** "Def Party" (Get Off Me Records FAP-002) 1987

14 **Dominating MC's** "Knowledge Bound" (Pay-Hill Records DMC 001) date unknown
Photography: Scott Shepard

15 **The Mix Crew** "Black Leather" (Jammin' Jim Records) 1987

16 **Left and Right Shoe M.C.'s Featuring D.J. Rated "X"** "Get Funky and Get Loose"
(Talking Horse Records THP-002) 1988

17 **The Unknown DJ and DJ Slip** "Revenge of the X-Men" (Techno Kut Records TK-1204) 1988
Artwork: Darryl "Lyrrad" Davis

18 **E.V.I.A.N.** "Techno City" (Techno Kut Records TK-1206) 1988
Artwork: Daryl "Lyrrad" Davis

19 **Mic Bay B** "Washed Up" (no label) date unknown

20 **Neil Young** *On the Beach* (Reprise Records R 2180) 1974

COVER STORY 02 Andrew Mason

01 **Sun Ra and the Arkestra** *Sound of Joy* (Delmark DS-414) 1968
Design and photography: Zbigniew Jastrzebski

02 **El Gran Combo** *Los Nenes Sicodelicos* (Gema LPG-3066) 1968

03 **Barrabas** *Barrabas* (RCA APLI 0219) 1972

04 **Sweetwater** *Melon* (Reprise 6473) 1971
Photography and concept: Anette Del Zoppo; tie-dye: Carol Lee

05 **"The Executioner"** *Dangerous* (label unknown SRT-O59) date unknown

06 **Babe Ruth** *First Base* (Harvest SW-11151) 1973
Design, painting, and photography: Roger Dean

07 **Various Artists** *Floro Manco Presenta—Salsaaa!!!* (Palacio LP 7248) date unknown

08 **Freddie McCoy** *Peas 'N' Rice* (Prestige 7487) 1965
Design: Mary Jo Schwalbach

09 **Don Cherry** *Organic Music Society* (Caprice RIKS LP44,50) 1972

10 **Canseira & Marimbondo** *Encontro De Cobras Criadas* (Tapecar TC.085) date unknown
Design and photography: Joselito

11 **Linval Thompson, Wayne Jarrett, and Ranking Trevor** *Train to Zion Dub* (Tuff Gong) 1981
Design: Neville Garrick

12 **Gilberto Gil** *Gilberto Gil* (Polygram) 1968
Design: Rogério Duarte, Antônio Dias, and David Drew Zingg

13 **Ugly Man** *Ugly Lover* (Sunset Records) 1985
Design and artwork: Orville "Bagga" Case—The Inkspot Ltd.

14 **Ornette Coleman Quartet** *This Is Our Music* (Atlantic 1353) 1960
Design: Loring Eutemey; photograpy: Lee Friedlander

15 **Various Artists** *The Rap Pack* (Fresh Records LPRE-003) 1987
Art direction: Meddling Mendel; artwork: Isaiah Roberts

16 **The Brothers** "Brothers/ I Got Rhythm" (B-Boy Records) 1987

17 **Hubert Laws** *Family* (Columbia JC 36396) 1980
Photography: Art Kane

18 **Willie Colón & Rubén Blades** *Siembra* (Fania JMOO-537) 1978
Photography: J. P. Posse; art and illustration: Irene Perlicz

19 **The Voices of East Harlem** *Right On Be Free* (Elektra EKS-74080) date unknown
Photography: Jan Bloom, Bruce Davidson, and Carl Samrock

20 **Various Artists** *It's a Family Affair* (ECR-GARD Records CG 70598) date unknown

COVER STORY 03 Oliver Wang

01   **The Howard Hanger Trio** *A Child Is Born* (Trav MLSP-2250) date unknown
Photography: J. Allen/Flair Photographic

02   **Joe Bataán** *Salsoul* (Mericana Records XMS-124) 1973
Art and design: QuinGraphic Productions Inc.

03   **Willie Colón** *Cosa Nuestra* (Fania SLP 384) 1972
Design: Izzy Sanabria; photography: Henri Wolfe

04   **King T** *Act a Fool* (Capitol C1-90544) 1988
Photography: Glen E. Friedman

05   **Weldon Irvine** *Liberated Brother* (Nodlew Music 1001T) 1972
Design: Keith Collins; photography: Darnell Mitchell

06   **Roberto Roena** *Roberto Roena y Su Apollo Sound 5* (International Records SLP 00443) 1973
Design: We=? Graphic Design, Inc; Walter Velez/Izzy Sanabria

07   **Charles Wright & the Watts 103rd Street Rhythm Band** *Express Yourself* (Warner Brothers 1864) 1970
Art direction: Ed Thrasher; illustration: Mark English

08   **Har You Percussion Group** *Har You Percussion Group* (ESP Disk ESP 1067) 1969
Art: Dan Prothero of Fog City Graphics

09   **The Radio Light Orchestras of Switzerland** *Lightly Swiss – Music for Christmas* (Swiss Broadcasting Company)
Design: Jean Ducommun and Colin Farmer

10   **Toro** *Toro* (Coco Records CLP 106) 1975
Design: Chico Alvarez; illustration: Walter Velez

11   **A Tribe Called Quest** *People's Instinctive Travels and the Paths of Rhythm* (Jive Records 1331-1-J) 1990
Illustration: Paije Hunyady and Bryant Peters

12   **De La Soul** *De La Soul Is Dead* (Tommy Boy TB 1041) 1991
Illustration: Joseph Buckingham

13   **Enrique Lynch y Su Conjunto** *Bomba Tropical* (Discos Sono Radio S.E. 9412)
Photography: Guillermo Fowks, model: Zelmira Aguilar

14   **Betty Davis** *Betty Davis* (Just Sunshine Records JSS-5) 1973
Design and type: Ron Levine; photography: Mel Dixon

15   **Quinn Harris and the Masterminds** *All in the Soul* (Reynolds Records PR-711) 1970

16   **Larry T. and the Family** *I'm Moving On* (LET Music LT 301) 1979
Design: Susan I. Tully; layout: Larry Thompson

17   **Sarah Webster Fabio** *Jujus/Alchemy of the Blues* (Folkways Records FL 9714) 1976
Design: Ronald Clyne

18   **S.O.U.L.** *Can You Feel It* (Musicor MS 3230) 1972
Photography: Richard Talmadge

19   **Cookie Wong** *Bad Talk* (Penthouse Records JA 3-26-36) 1977

20   **Bappi Lahiri** *Morchha: Confrontation of Action with Reaction* (Polydor of India 2392 202) 1980

COVER STORY 04 Brian DiGenti

01 **Lemuria** *Lemuria* (Heaven Records AL 00001) 1978

02 **Afrosound** *La Danza de los Mirlos* (Discos Fuentes 200870) 1973

03 *Attaining Cosmic Consciousness* (Rosicrucian Recordings) date unknown

04 **Iz** "Brainwash/ The Bomb" (AMP Records 1233001) 1983
Design: Philco and Courtney Branch; logo design: Courtney Branch; logo artwork: Nancy Lujan

05 **Michel Herr, Bill Frisell, Vinton Johnson, and Kermit Driscoll** *Good Buddies* (EMI/Shiva 1A 064-63568) 1979
Design: Studio Visions Kitou; painting: Roland Delcol

06 **Les Baxter** *The Dunwich Horror Original Motion Picture Soundtrack* (Varèse Sarabande VC 81103) 1979

07 **Eugene McDaniels** *Headless Heroes of the Apocalypse* (Atlantic Records SD 8281) 1971
Graphic design: Tomas Nittner; photography: Bill del Conte; painting: Harvey Konigsberg

08 **IAM** *L'Ecole du Micro D'Argent* (Delabel /243 8 44000 1 9) 1997
Artwork: Tous des K

09 **Phil Moore Jr.** *Right On* (Atlantic Records SD 1530) 1969
Design: Haig Adishian; photography: Fred Seligo

10 **The Larks** *Soul Kaleidoscope* (Money Records MS 1107) circa 1970
Design: Erroll Dolphin; photography by Lawrence Heywood

11 **Bubbha Thomas** *Life & Times* (Lightin' Records 2004) 1985
Design: William Thomas II; photography: Frank Martin

12 **James Polk & Co.** *You Know the Feeling...!* (Trilogy Records TP 100) 1982
Design: Frank Polk

13 **Kit Ream** *All that I Am* (Creative Records MW 1001) 1978
Artwork: Kit Ream

14 **DJ Krush** *Strictly Turntablized* (Mo' Wax MW LP 025) 1994
Design: Swifty; cover art: Futura 2000; Krush logo: Ben Drury

15 **Galt MacDermot** *Ghetto Suite* (Kilmarnock Records KIL 72002) 1972
Design by Milographics; photography: Tom Lesley

16 **Soul Generation** *Beyond Body and Soul* (Ebony Record ES-2000) 1972
Design and photography: Allen Breslow

17 **Stairsteps** *Stairsteps* (Buddha Records BDS 5079) 1971
Photography: Maurer Productions

18 **Universal Jones** *Vol. 1* (MGM/Verve Records MV 5084) 1972
Art direction: Steve Kursh; photography: Vince Aiosa

19 **The Cheebacabra** *Metamorphosis* (Mackrosoft MS 0007) 2003
Design: Tom Manning and Leroy Smits; cover image: *The Perception Epic*, copyright 1981: Daved Levitan

20 **Wilson Simonal** *Simonal* (Odeon MOFB 3643) 1970
Design and artwork: Sapia, Urano, and Prosperi

COVER STORY 05 Matt Rogers

01   **Jimmy Castor Bunch** *It's Just Begun* (RCA LSP-4640) 1972
      Design: Frank Mulvey; art direction: Acy Lehman; artwork: Corrigan

02   **Mandrill** *Mandrilland* (Polydor PD2-9002) 1974
      Artwork: Goodman Gries

03   **War** *The World Is a Ghetto* (United Artist Records UAS-5652) 1972
      Design: Howard Miller

04   **James Brown** *Hell* (Polydor PD2-9001) 1974
      Design: Ted Pettus, Kameny Associates, Inc.; artwork: Joe Belt

05   **Jimmy McGriff and Groove Holmes** *Giants of the Organ in Concert* (Groove Merchant GM 3300) 1973
      Art direction: Sam Alexander; photography: Roy Di Tosti

06   **El Chicano** *Revolución* (Kapp Records KS 3640) 1971
      Design: Virginia Clark; art direction: John C. LePrevost; photography: Eddie Caballero

07   **Roberta Flack** *First Take* (Atlantic Records SD 8230) 1969
      Design: Stanislaw Zagorski; photography: Ken Heinen

08   **Ramsey Lewis** *Back to the Roots* (Cadet CA-60001) 1971
      Art and design: Jim O'Connell

09   **Dramatics** *Watcha See Is Watcha Get* (Volt VOS-6018) 1972
      Design: Ron Gorden; illustration: Neil Deckert

10   **The Watts 103rd Street Rhythm Band** *Together* (Warner Brothers WS1761) 1968
      Design: Bob Zoell; art direction: Ed Thrasher

11   **Boogaloo Joe Jones** *No Way!* (Prestige PR 10004) 1971
      Design and photography: Don Schlitten

12   **Afrique** *Soul Makossa* (Mainstream 394) 1973

13   **Tito Rodriguez** *Palladium Memories* (TR Records TLP-00200) 1970

14   **La Lupe** *La Lupe es La Reina* (Tico Records LP-1192) 1969
      Design: Ely Besalel; photography: Warren Flagler

15   **Sharon Jones and the Dap-Kings** *Naturally* (Daptone DAP-004) 2005
      Art direction: David Serre; photography: Dulce Pinzon

16   **Aretha Franklin** *Live at Filmore West* (Atlantic SD 7205) 1971
      Design: Tom Wilkes; photography: Jim Marshall

17   **Bob Marley and the Wailers** *Catch a Fire* (Island Records ILPS 9241) 1973
      Artwork: John Bonis of CCS; photography: Esther Anderson

18   **Albert King** *I Wanna Get Funky* (Stax MPS-8536) 1973/1974
      Art Direction: Davis Fried Krieger Inc.; creative direction: Larry Shaw and Ron Gordon; photography: Maldwin Hamlin

19   **George Freeman** *Man & Woman* (Groove Merchant GM3305) 1974
      Design: David Lartaud; art direction: Frank Daniel; photography: Manuel Gonzales

20   **O'Donel Levy** *Everything I Do Gonna Be Funky* (Groove Merchant GM535) 1974
      Design: David Lartaud; art direction: Frank Daniel; photography: Manny Gonzales

COVER STORY 06 Dante Carfagna

01 **Terry Reid** *River* (Atlantic ST-7259) 1973
Design and photography: Camouflage Productions

02 **Sweet Slag** *Sweet Slag* (President PTLS-1042) 1971
Art and photography: Nadia Bambridge

03 **Harry Bertoia** "Gong Gong/ Elemental" (Sonambient FW-1026) date unknown

04 **Horde Catalytique Pour La Fin** *Horde Catalytique Pour La Fin* (Futura SON-03) 1971
Design: Zia Mirabdolbaghi; photography: Alain Sabatier

05 **Karen Dalton** *It's So Hard to Tell Who's Going to Love You the Best* (Capitol ST-271) 1969
Design: Dave Krieger; photography: Joel Brodsky

06 **James Knight & the Butlers** *Black Knight* (Cat 711) date unknown
Photography: Peter Nashick

07 **Il Gruppo** *Private Sea of Dreams* (RCA-Victor LSP-3846) 1967
Photography: David B. Hecht

08 **Dennis Olivieri** *Come to the Party* (VMC VS-130) date unknown

09 **The Paris Smith Quartet** *Thought Seeds* (Oracle 1083) 1983
Art and design: Carol Sawall

10 *Sound Communication by the Bottlenosed Dolphin* (Leprechaun 1) 1978
Art and design: Janes Spottswood Keller Caldwell

11 **Furekaaben** *Prinsessevaerelset* (Spectator SL-1017) 1970
Design: Furekaaben; photography: Torbjorn Thomsen

12 **John Bayley** *Minstrel of the Morning* (Lifetime Records 2001) 1976
Design: John C. Bayley; photography: Alan Schlosser

13 **Mark III** *Marvin Whoremonger* (Blacklite Records BT-7001) 1976
Art direction: Cholly Williams

14 **Woodbine** *Roots* (Blue Hour BH-1010) 1971
Design: Jim Price; artwork: David Staff

15 **Erica Pomerance** *You Used to Think* (ESP-Disk 1099) 1968
Artwork: David Syversen

16 **Various Artists** *Joint Effort* (Century 33642) 1969
Art and design: Phyl Herschel and Debbie Richards

17 **Coyote** *Coyote* (Beuna Suerte BSR-1034) date unknown
Design: Maravilla; photography: Herbert Acevedo

18 **Little Howling Wolf** *The Guardian* (Solidarity) 1982

19 **Collie Ryan** *The Giving Tree* (Colorado River Gold Mining Co. CRGMC-1) 1973
Art and design: Collie Ryan

20 **Purple Image** *Purple Image* (Map City MAP-3015) date unknown
Art and design: Michael Kanarek

COVER STORY 07 Robbie Busch

01   **Sparrow's Troubadours** *Hot & Sweet* (RA 2140) 1969
      Design: Lee-Myles Assoc. Inc. NYC

02   **Various Artists** *Mambo for Cats* (RCA Victor LMP-1063) 1955
      Design: Jim Flora; artwork: Jim Flora

03   **Arzachel** *Arzachel* (Roulette Records) 1969
      Design: Dave Stewart; artwork: Dave Stewart

04   **Coke** *Coke* (Sound Triangle 7773) 1972
      Design: Drago

05   **Chakachas** *Chakachas* (Avco AV-11005) 1967
      Design: Maurer Productions; photography: Lisa Little, Museum of Primitive Art, New York

06   **Gary Panter** *Pray for Smurph* (Overheat Records OH-0001) 1983
      Design: Gary Panter; artwork: Gary Panter

07   **Screamin' Jay Hawkins** *Because Is In Your Mind (Armpitrubber)* (Phillips PHO 600 336) 1970
      Artwork: Karl Wirsum, the Art Institute of Chicago

08   **Joe Coleman** *Internal Machine* (Blast First FU10) 1990
      Artwork: Joe Coleman

09   **Tom Wilson** *All-American Boy* (Aboveground Records Inc. AR102) 1983
      Design and photography: Lloyd Buddy Mailander; type: Duke T&E Services, Inc.

10   **West Street Mob** *Break Dance/Electric Boogie* (Sugarhill Records SH 9201) 1984
      Design: Hemu Aggarwal, AQ Graphics Inc.; photography: Todd Roskin

11   **Mark-Ski** *Rappin' and Rockin'* (Independent Record Maker) 1982
      Design and artwork: Mark Ski

12   **Rev. Jasper Williams** *I Fell in Love with a Prostitute* (Church Door Records LP 1001) date unknown

13   **Die Schwestern and Brüder vom Kegelklub** *Gut Holz!/Bowling Time*
      (Royal Sound OLE 14000 P) date unknown
      Photography: Janke

14   **Liz Dargan and the Gospelettes** *Everything's Gonna Be Alright* (Songbird/ABC SBLP-229) 1973
      Photography: Bernard Nagler

15   **Sunny & the Sunliners** *The Missing Link* (Key-Loc KL 3010) date unknown

16   **Jimmy Cliff** *The Harder They Come* (Mango MLPS-9202) 1972
      Design: CCS Associates

17   **Tito Ramos** *Where My Head Is At* (Cotique CS 1069) 1972
      Design and illustration: Ray Mulett

18   **Pucho and the Latin Soul Brothers** *Super Freak* (Zanzee SZLP 2603) 1972
      Design: Ron Lucas; artwork: Floyd Sowell of Environmental Forms, Inc.

19   **My Bloody Valentine** *Untitled (Feed Me With Your Kiss)* (Creation CRE 061T) 1988

20   **Serge Gainsbourg** *Love on the Beat* (Phillips PHL 1 3006) 1984
      Photography: William Klein

COVER STORY 08 Amir Abdullah

01 **Brother Jack McDuff** *Down Home Style* (Blue Note BST 84322) 1969
Art direction: Frank Gauna

02 **Mongo Santamaria** *Sofrito* (Vaya JMVS-53) 1976
Design: Ron Levine; photography: Lee Marshall

03 **Horace Silver Quintet** *6 Pieces of Silver* (Blue Note BLP 1539) 1956
Design: Reid Miles; photography: Francis Wolff

04 **Horace Silver Quintet** *The Stylings of Silver* (Blue Note BLP 1562) 1957
Photography: Francis Wolff

05 **Magnum** *Fully Loaded* (The Phoenix LP 6001) date unknown

06 **The Lyman Woodard Organization** *Saturday Night Special* (Strata Records SRI-105-75) 1975
Design: John Sinclair and Lyman Woodard; art direction: John Sinclair; photography: Leni Sinclair

07 **Mtume** *Kiss the World Goodbye* (Epic 35255) 1978
Art: Stanley Fawkes Burnside

08 **Michael White's Magic Music Company** *Go with the Flow* (ABC Records ASD-9281) date unknown
Illustration: Keith Washington

09 **Henry Debich's Orkiestra Polskiego** *String Beat* (Muza SX 1276) 1975
Art: J. Flisak

10 **Splash** *Splash* (PLA 3001) 1974
Design: Ardy Strüwer

11 **Jimmy Smith** *At the Organ Vol. 2* (Blue Note BLP 1552) 1958
Design: Reid Miles; photography: Francis Wolff

12 **Jimmy Smith** *Root Down – Jimmy Smith Live!* (Verve V6-8806) 1972
Photography: David Rawcliffe

13 **Ralfi Pagan** *I Can See* (Fania Series 0598) 1975
Design concept: Clarence V. Dallas Jr.; design: Anthony Troutman; photography: John W. Marsh

14 **Leon Ware** *Musical Massage* (Gordy G6-976S1) 1976
Art direction: Frank Mulvey; photography: Sam Emerson

15 **Oscar Peterson** *The Jazz Soul of Oscar Peterson* (Verve MG VS-68351) 1959
Art director: Merle Shore; artwork: Bill Kinser

16 **JJ Band** *JJ Band* (CBS 64396) 1971
Photography: Hans and Toto Kellerman

17 **McCoy Tyner** *Today and Tomorrow* (Impulse! A-63) 1963
Design: Robert Flynn/Viceroy; photography: Jim Marshall

18 **McCoy Tyner Trio with Roy Haynes and Henry Grimes** *Reaching Fourth* (Impulse! A-33) 1963
Design: Robert Flynn/Viceroy; photography: Bob Ghiraldini

19 **Jorge Dalto** *Chevere* (United Artists UA-LA671-G) 1976
Design: Bill Burks; art direction: Ria Lewerke; illustration: Steve Smith

20 **Creation** *Creation* (Atco Records SD 7041) date unknown
Concept and design: Pacific Eye & Ear; illustration: Drew Struzan and Bill Garland

COVER STORY 09 John Paul Jones

01 **The Polyphonics** *Zounds! What Sounds* (CMI 110) date unknown
Photography: Harry Farmlett

02 **The Treacherous Three** *The Treacherous Three* (Sugarhill Records SH 9124) 1984
Design and production: AQ Graphics, Inc.; photography: Hemu Aggarwal

03 **William Onyeabor** *Atomic Bomb* (Wilfilms Limited WRLP 1002) 1978

04 **Roland Kirk** *The Inflated Tear* (Atlantic SC 1502) 1968
Design: Stanislaw Zagorski; photography: Lee Friedlander

05 **City Boys Band** *Nya Asem Hwe* (Diram LDR 2001) 1977
Design: Dan A. Opoku; photography: Studio Fred Attoh

06 **Ofege** *Higher Plane Breeze* (Polydor POLP-015) 1977
Design: Poatson Maboju

07 **Johnny Adams** *Heart & Soul* (SSS International Records SSS #5) 1969

08 **Joe Bataan** *Mr. New York and the East Side Kids* (Fania LP 395) 1971
Design: Izzy Sanabria; photography: Len Dauman

09 **Cedric IM Brooks** *One Essence* (High Note) 1977

10 **Survival** *Simmer Down* (ARC 001) 1977

11 **TNT Boys** *Sex Symbols (Simbolos Sexuales)* (Cotique C-1038) date unknown
Design: Izzy Sanabria; photography: Bradley Olman

12 **Jorge Lopez Ruiz** *Amor Buenos Aires* (Catalyst CAT-7908) 1977
Design: David Lartaud

13 **Lightnin' Hopkins** *"Live" at the Bird Lounge* (Guest Star G 1450) 1969

14 **Lynnfield Pioneers** *Free Popcorn* (Matador OLE-342) 1999
Collage/illustration: John Mathias; lettering: Glen Elf

15 **Djinns Music** *Exode Rural* (Discogram DISCO 006) 1978
Photography: Ziagnon Dobre

16 **Sledge Funk Band** *Black Children* (RTS Records RTLPS 017) 1978

17 **Scorpion** *Scorpion* (Tower ST-5171) 1969
Design: Roy Steyskal

18 **Various Artists** *EMI Super Hits Vol. 2* (EMI HNLX 5208) 1982
Design: Mohammed Arahi; artwork: Kolorgrafiks Studio

19 **Jade Stone & Luv** *Mosaics – Pieces of Stone* (Jade Records JS 4351) 1977
Artwork: Charles Hooper

20 **The Family Tree** *Miss Butters* (RCA/Victor LPM-3955) 1968
Illustration: Dick Hendler

COVER STORY 10 Jeff Mao

01 **Sir William Portis, Jr. and the Elements of Sound** *By the Time I Get to Phoenix* (Reelsound P&B 7120) date unknown

02 **U.S. Atlantic Fleet Navy Show Band** *Hand Clappin' Music* (U.S. Navy promotional record) date unknown
Design: Herbert E. Jones, Jr.

03 **TNT** *Hotter than Hell* (King Quality Records KQ6) 1989
Photography: J. Lash; artwork: Scratch

04 **L.A. Dream Team** "Rudy and Snake" (MCA 23793) 1987
Design: Georgopoulos/Imada; writing on cover: Jonathan Shecter, September 1987

05 **Dadisi Komolafe** *Hassan's Walk* (Nimbus NS-3035) 1983
Design and photography: Michael D. Wilcots

06 **Various Artists** *Latin Africa* (Discolor LP-092) 1975
Design: Ernesto Alonso

07 **Lamont Dozier** *Love and Beauty* (Invictus KZ 33134) 1975
Design: Ed Lee and Gerard Huerta; photography: Don Hunstein

08 **The Edge of Daybreak** *Eyes of Love* (Bohannon's 005074) date unknown
Design: George R. Fugate

09 **Mob Style** *The Good, the Bad, the Ugly* (Grove St. GRS123) 1991

10 **Various Artists** *In Full Effect!!! Cleveland Style* (Oh.10 Records) 1988
Design: BMR Productions; cover concept: Mr. Boss; illustration: Sano D.E.F.; photography: Beatrice Grier/Bob Simpson

11 **Michael Longo** *900 Shades of the Blues* (Groove Merchant GM3304) 1975
Design: Frank Daniel; photography: Chuck Stewart

12 **Luis Santi y su Conjunto** *El Bigote* (Sound Triangle STS-8000) date unknown
Design: Cinestudio

13 **Rappermatical 5** "Party People" (Dynamite Pep 1002) 1980

14 **The Outlaw Four** "Million Dollar Legs" (Dynamite Pep 1001) 1980

15 **The Meters** *Look-Ka Py Py* (Josie 4011) 1970
Design and photography: the Graffiteria; art supervision: Janie Gans;
writing on cover: Pat Simpson, circa 1972

16 **James Mason** *Rhythm of Life* (Chiaroscuro CR 189) 1977
Design: Ron Warwell; concept: James Mason; airbrush coloring: Karl Blickenderfer;
photography: Rollo Phlecks; writing on cover: Unknown, June 1978

17 **Big Lu Valeny y Los Muchachos** *Un Amigo Borracho* (Buena Suerte BSR-1031) 1972

18 **James Rivers** *Thrill Me* (J.B.'s JB-101) date unknown
Design: Senator Jones; photography: Bill Synegal

19 **Ray Terrace** *Oye El Cuchy Frito Man* (Jubilee 7002) 1965
Photography: Bob Stephens

20 **Al Escobar and His Orchestra** *El Sonido Moderno De/The Modern Sounds Of* (Tico 1184) 1969

COVER STORY 11 Andre Torres

01 **Boy Wonder Crusade and Miracle Revival Fellowship Choirs** *The Flesh Is a Mess* (no label) date unknown
Photography: Samuel King

02 **Christ-Win's Band** *Smokin' Crack* (C-Win's Records LP-102) date unknown
Design: Etheridge Lovett

03 **Lionel Hampton** *Off into a Black Thing* (Brunswick Records BL 7-54213) 1976
Design: N.B. Ward Assoc.; art direction: Carl Napoletano; lettering design: Harve Kossoff

04 **The Black Voices** *On the Streets in Watts* (Ala Records) 1970
Design: Howard Goldstein; photography: Dominic Belmonte

05 **Chuck Brown and the Soul Searchers** *Bustin' Loose* (Source Records SOR-3076) 1979
Design: Dancer Productions, Ltd.; art: Ark Wong

06 **Kawaida** *Kawaida* (O'Be Records OB-301) 1970
Art direction: Peter Weir; photo: Martin Bough

07 **Nina Simone** *Nina Simone* (Up Front Records UPF-145) date unknown

08 **Duke Ellington** *The Afro-Eurasian Eclipse* (Fantasy Records F-9498) 1975
Art direction: Phil Carroll

09 **Jimmy McGriff** *Groove Grease* (Groove Merchant Records GM-503) 1971
Art direction: Daniel Cooper-Bey; photography: Chuck Stewart

10 **Fela Ransome-Kuti and the Africa '70** *Shakara* (Editions Makossa EM2305) 1974
Design: Africa 70 Organisation; photography: Africa 70 Agency

11 **Melvin Van Peebles** *Sweet Sweetback's Baadasssss Song OST* (Stax Records STS-3001) 1971

12 **The Cecil Holmes Soulful Sounds** *The Black Motion Picture Experience* (Buddha Records BDS-5129) 1973
Art direction: Glen Christensen; packaging: Milton Sincoff

13 **Burning Spear** *Man In the Hills* (Island Records ILPS-9412) 1976
Design and illustration: Neville Garrick

14 **Charles Earland** *Leaving this Planet* (Prestige Records P-66002) 1974
Design: Tony Lane, illustration: Dave Hubbard

15 **Dwana** *Dwana* (Caytronics Records CYS-1312) 1972
Art direction: Manuel Vega F.

16 **Jimmy McGriff** *Black Pearl* (United Artists Records BST-84374) 1971
Art direction: Norman Seeff; illustration: John Van Hamersveld

17 **Port Authority** *Port Authority* (U.S. Navy 71001) 1971
Design: Grey & Davis Inc.; photography: Stasolla & Tesoro, Inc.

18 **Ira Sullivan** *Strings Attached* (Pausa Records PR-7169) 1985
Design: Iris Massey

19 **La Fantastica** *From Ear to Ear* (Ghetto Records SG-0014) 1971
Design: Rafael Mulett; illustration: Charlie Rosario

20 **The Nazty** *I Got to Move* (Nashboro Records, Mankind 206) 1976
Design: Dan Quest & Associates, Inc.

COVER STORY 12 Brian "B+" Cross

01 **Paul Humphrey** *America Wake Up* (Blue Thumb Records BTS 66) 1973
Design and photography: Barry Feinstein for Camouflage Productions

02 **Commander William Guy Carr** *Pawns in the Game* (American United Records AU-16) date unknown

03 **Harry J Allstars** *Liquidator* (Trojan Records TBL 104) 1969
Design: C.C.S. Advertising Associates; photography: Ged Grimmel

04 **Quilapayun** *Basta* (JotaJota Records JJ-07) date unknown

05 **Various Artists** *Smash Internment: Live Recording in Long Kesh* (R&O Records ROL 3002) 1972

06 **Milton Nascimento** *Clube Da Esquina* (EMI-Odeon 31C 164 422901/2) 1972

07 **Andrew Hill** *Grass Roots* (Blue Note BST 84303) 1968
Photography: Jordan Malek

08 **The Clash** *Sandinista Now!* (Epic AS 913) 1980

09 **Willey Von Huff-n-Puff** *F.L.E.X. (Friends, Lovers & Estranged X's)* (Protocol Entertainment Group) 1982

10 **Ali Mohamed Birra with the Adu Band** *Ali Mohamed Birra with the Adu Band* (Kaifa Records LPKF17) 1975

11 **The Palo Alto High School Jazz Ensemble** *Big Band '73* (Custom Fidelity CFS-3198) 1973
Design: George Glover; art direction: Nita Morris; photography direction: Greg Tseng

12 **The Admiral Dele Abiodun and His Top Hitters Band** *Adawa Super Sound* (Olumo Records OPRS 21) 1975

13 **Various Artists** *The Guitar and the Gun: A Collection of Ghanaian Highlife Dance Music*
 (Africagram Records LP3 35 404 018) 1983
Artwork: Ja Mesphe-Lan; photography: Eddie Bru-Mindah

14 **Various Artists** *Nordeste: Cordel, Repente, Canção* (Tapecar TC-50) 1975
Art direction: Aluízio Falcão; artwork: J. Borges

15 **The Three Sounds** *Three Moods* (Limelight LS 86014) 1965
Design and photography: Daniel Czubak

16 **Dub Specialist** *Mellow Dub* (Coxsone FCD 7725) 1974

17 **Krishnanda** *Krishnanda* (CBS 37564) 1968

18 **Xingu** *Cantos e Ritmos* (Phillips 6349 022) 1972
Cover: Aldo Luiz

19 **Preto Vehlo** *Hinos e Pontos de Umbanda* (AMCLP 5074)
Cover: Gilson A. Teixeira; layout: Gilliat Pinto

20 **Eazy-E** *It's On (Dr. Dre) 187um Killa* (Ruthless Records 88561-5503-1) 1993
Design: Allan Wai; art direction: Dave Bett; artwerk: Eazy-E; photography: B+

**ARRIVE
FRESH**

**LISTEN
CAREFULLY**

**STAY
SMOOTH**